GOD WITH US

REFLECTIONS ON THE INCARNATION

Charles Spurgeon

GLH Publishing

LOUISVILLE, KY

Originally Titled: *Christ's Incarnation: The Foundation of Christianity*.
Passmore and Alabaster, 1901.

GLH Publishing Edition, 2019

ISBN:
  Paperback 978-1-948648-85-1

CONTENTS

I. THE ANGELS' SONG, ITS OPENING NOTE

"GLORY *to God in the highest.*" The instructive lesson to be learned from this opening note of the angels' song is, that salvation is God's highest glory. He is glorified in every dewdrop that twinkles in the morning sunshine. He is magnified in every wood flower that blossoms in the copse, although it is born to blush unseen of man, and may seem to waste its sweetness on the forest air. God is glorified in every bird that warbles on the trees, and in every lamb that skips in the meadows. Do not the fishes in the sea praise Him? From the tiny minnow to the huge leviathan, do not all creatures that swim in the waters laud and magnify His great Name? Do not all created things extol Him? Is there aught beneath the sky, save man, that doth not glorify God? Do not the stars exalt Him, when they write His Name in golden letters upon the azure of heaven? Do not the lightnings adore Him when they flash His brightness in arrows of light piercing the midnight darkness? Do not the thunderpeals extol Him when they roll like drums in the march of the God of armies? Do not all things that He hath made, from the least even to the greatest, exalt Him?

But sing, sing, O universe, till thou hast exhausted thyself, yet thou canst not chant an anthem so sweet as the song of Incarnation! Though Creation may be a majestic organ of praise, it cannot reach the compass of the golden canticle,—Incarnation! There is more melody in Jesus in the

1

manger than in the whole sublime oratorio of the
Creation. There is more grandeur in the song that
heralds the birth of the Babe of Bethlehem than
there is in worlds on worlds rolling in silent grandeur around the throne of the Most High.

Pause, reader, for a minute, and consider this
great truth. See how every one of the Divine attributes is here magnified. Lo, what *wisdom* is here!
The Eternal becomes man in order that God may
be just, and yet be the Justifier of him that believeth in Jesus. What *power* also is here, for where
is power so great as when it concealeth itself?
What power, that God should unrobe Himself for
a while, and become man! Behold, too, what *love*
is thus revealed to us when Jesus becomes a man;
and what *faithfulness!* How many promises and
prophecies are this day fulfilled! How many solemn obligations are this hour discharged! Tell me
one attribute of God that you say is not manifest in
Jesus; and your ignorance shall be to me the reason why you have not seen it to be so. The whole
of God is glorified in Christ; and though some part
of the Name of God is written in the material universe, it is best read in Him who was the Son of
man, and also the Son of God.

II. THE ANGELS' SONG, THE ADDED STANZA

"GLORY to God in the highest," was an old, old song to the angels; they had sung that strain before the foundation of the world. But, now, they sang as it were a new song before the throne of God, and in the ears of mortal men, for they added this stanza, "*and on earth peace.*"

They did not sing like that in the Garden of Eden. There was peace there, but it seemed to be a matter of course, and to be a thing scarcely needing to be mentioned in their song. There was more than peace there, for there was also glory to God. But man had fallen, and since the day when the Lord God drove him out of Eden, and placed the cherubim with a flaming sword which turned every way, to keep the way of the tree of life, there had been no peace on earth, save in the breasts of believers, who had obtained peace of heart and conscience even from the promise of the Incarnation of Christ.

Wars had raged unto the ends of the earth; men had slaughtered one another, heaps on heaps. There had been strife within as well as struggles without. Conscience had fought with man, and Satan had tormented him with sinful thoughts. There had been no peace on earth since Adam fell.

But, now, when the new-born King made His appearance, the swaddling-band with which He was wrapped up was the white flag of peace. That manger was the place where the treaty was signed, whereby warfare should be stopped between man's conscience and himself, and between man's conscience and his God. Then it was that the trumpet of the heavenly herald was blown aloud, and the royal proclamation was made, "Sheathe thy sword, O man, sheathe thy sword, O conscience, for God has provided a way by which He can be at peace with man, and by which man can be at peace with God, and with his own conscience, too!"

The Gospel of the grace of God promises peace to every man who accepts it; where else can peace be found, but in the message of Jesus? And what a peace it is! It is like a river, and the righteousness of it is like the waves of the sea. It is "the peace of God, which passeth all understanding, which shall keep our hearts arid minds through Christ Jesus." This sacred peace between the soul pardoned and God the Pardoner, this marvellous "at-one-ment" between the guilty sinner and his righteous Judge, this it was of which the angels sang when they said, "Peace on earth."

III. THE ANGELS' SONG, ITS FINAL NOTE

"GOOD *will toward men*." Wise men have thought, from what they have seen in Creation, that God had much good will toward men, or else His works would never have been so constructed as they are for their comfort; yet I never heard of any man who was willing to risk his soul's salvation upon such a faint hope as that. But I have not only heard of thousands, I know thousands, who are quite sure that God has good will toward men; and if you ask them the reason for their confidence, they will give you a full and satisfactory answer. They will say, "God has good will toward men, for He gave His Son to die for them." No greater proof of kindness between the Creator and His subjects can possibly be afforded than when the Creator gives His only-begotten and well-beloved Son to die in the place and stead of guilty sinners.

Though the first note of the angels' song is Godlike, and though the second note is peaceful, this third note melts my heart the most. Some seem to think of God as if He were an austere being who hated all mankind. Others picture Him as a mere abstraction, taking no interest in our affairs. But this angelic message assures us that God has "good will toward men."

You know what "good will" means. Well, all that it means, and more, God has to you, ye sons and daughters of Adam. Poor sinner, thou hast broken His laws; thou art half afraid to come to the throne of His mercy, lest He should spurn thee;

5

hear thou this, and be comforted, — God has good will toward men, so good a will that He has said, and said it with an oath, too, "As I live, saith the Lord God, I have no pleasure in the death of the wicked; but that the wicked turn from his way and live;" — so good a will, moreover, that He has even condescended to say, "Come now, and let us reason together, saith the Lord: though your sins be as scarlet, they shall be as white as snow; though they be red like crimson, they shall be as wool." And if you say, "Lord, how shall I know that Thou hast this good will towards me," He points to the manger, and says, "Sinner, if I had not had good will towards thee, would I have parted with My beloved Son? If I had not had good will towards the human race, would I have given up My Son to become one of that race, that He might, by so doing, redeem from death as many of them as would believe on Him?

Ye who doubt the love of God to guilty men, look away to that glorious circle of angels; see the blaze of glory lighting up the midnight sky; listen to their wondrous song, and let your doubts die in that sweet music, and be buried in a shroud of harmony. The angels' song assures us that God has good will toward men; He is willing to pardon; He does pass by iniquity, transgression, and sin. And if Satan shall try to insinuate such a doubt as this, "But though God hath good will toward men, yet He cannot violate His justice, therefore His mercy may be ineffective, and you may die;" then listen to that first note of the song, "Glory to God in the highest," and reply to Satan and all his temptations that, when God shows good will to a penitent sinner, there is not only peace in the sinner's heart and conscience, but glory is brought to every attribute of God, so He can be just, and yet justify the sinner who believeth in Jesus, and so glorify Himself while saving him.

IV. The Name of Jesus, God-Given

THE first angel, who appeared to the shepherds, gave them this message, "Fear not: for, behold, I bring you good tidings of great joy, which shall be to all people. For unto you is born this day in the city of David a Saviour, which is Christ the Lord." That word "Saviour" reminds us of what the angel of the Lord said to Joseph, "Fear not to take unto thee Mary thy wife: for that which is conceived in her is of the Holy Ghost. And she shall bring forth a Son, and thou shalt call His Name JESUS: for He shall save His people from their sins."

The condition of Joseph, when he heard this Name for the first time, is not altogether without instruction. The angel spake to him "in a dream." That Name is so soft and sweet that it breaks no man's rest, but rather yields a peace unrivalled, — "the peace of God." With such a dream, Joseph's sleep was even more blessed than his waking.

The Name of Jesus has evermore this power, for, to those who know its preciousness, it unveils a glory brighter than dreams have ever imaged. Under its wondrous spell, young men see visions, and old men dream dreams; and these do not mock them, as ordinary dreams do, but they are faithful and true prophecies of what shall surely come to pass. This Name brings before our minds a vision of glory, in the latter days, when Jesus shall reign from pole to pole; and yet another vision of glory unutterable when His people shall be

7

with Him where He is, and shall reign with Him
for ever and ever.

The Name of Jesus was comforting at the first
mention of it by the angel of the Lord, because of
the words with which it was accompanied; for
they were meant to remove perplexity and anxiety
from Joseph's mind. The angel said to him, "Fear
not;" and, truly, no name can banish fear like the
Name of Jesus; it is the beginning of hope, and the
end of despair.

It is worthy of note that the angel commenced
his message to the shepherds in a similar way:
"Fear not: for, behold, I bring you good tidings of
great joy." Let the sinner but hear of "a Saviour,
which is Christ the Lord," and, straightway, he
hopes to live, he rises out of the deadly lethargy of
his hopelessness, and, looking upward, he sees a
reconciled God, and fears no longer.

This Name of Jesus appears to us even more
full of rare delights when we meditate upon the
infinite preciousness of the glorious Person to
whom it was assigned. Ah, here is a Jonathan's
wood dripping with honey from every bough,
and he that tasteth it shall have his eyes enlight-
ened! We have no common Saviour, for neither
earth nor Heaven could produce His equal. At the
time when the Name was given to Him by God,
Jesus had not been seen by mortal eyes, for He lay
as yet concealed from human gaze; but soon He
came forth, having been born of Mary by the power of the Holy Ghost,—the matchless Holy Child
Jesus. He bore our nature, but not our corruption.
He was made in the likeness of sinful flesh, but
yet in His flesh there was no sin. He was "holy,
harmless, undefiled, separate from sinners." This
Holy One is the Son of God, and yet He is the Son
of man; this surpassing excellence of nature makes
His Name most precious.

V. The Name of Jesus, Prized by his People

The Name of Jesus, chosen by God for His Son, is also given to Him by all who truly know Him, and they give it to Him heartily, zealously, boldly. All of us call Him Jesus if we really know Him, and we are resolved to publish His Name abroad as long as we live. If He was Jesus in the cradle, what is He now that He is exalted in the highest heavens? As Emmanuel, God with us, His very Incarnation made Him Jesus, the Saviour of men; but what shall we say of Him now that, in addition to His Incarnation, we have His Atonement; and beside His Atonement, His Resurrection; and beyond that, His Ascension; and, to crown all, His perpetual Intercession?

How grandly does the title of Saviour befit Him now that He is able to save them to the uttermost that come unto God by Him, seeing He ever liveth to make intercession for them! If in the arms of His mother He was the Saviour, what is He now that He sitteth upon the throne of God? If wrapped in swaddling-bands He was Jesus, the Saviour, what is He now that the heavens have received Him? If in the workshop of Nazareth, and sitting in the temple among the doctors, He was Jesus, the Saviour, what is He now that His infancy and childhood are over, and He is exalted far above all principalities and powers? If He was Jesus when on the cross, presenting Himself as an offering for His people, what is He now that He hath by one sacrifice perfected for ever them that are set apart? What is He now that He sits at the right hand of God, expecting till His enemies be made His footstool?

Let all who trust in Him unite in calling our Lord by this tender human Name of Jesus. Did He not call all believers by the endearing titles of mother, and sister, and brother? Then we, too, will call Him Jesus.

> "Jesus, Name all names above,
>   Jesus best and nearest;
> Jesus, fount of perfect love,
>   Holiest, tenderest, dearest;
> Jesus, source of grace completed,
>   Jesus holiest, sweetest;
> Jesus, Saviour all Divine,
>   Thine's the Name, and only Thine."

VI. The Name of Jesus, Common, Yet Unique

The name Jesus was not at all uncommon among the Jews. Josephus mentions no less than twelve persons who bore that name. Salvation of a certain kind was so longed for by the Jews that their eagerness was seen even in the choice they made of their children's names. Their little ones were, because of their hopes concerning them, called saviours, yet they were not really saviours.

How common are nominal saviours! "Lo, here," say some, "is a saviour!" "Lo, there," cry others, "is another saviour!" All these have the name, but not the power; and now, our Lord Jesus Christ has claimed the title exclusively for Himself. His Name shall be called Jesus, for He alone is a Prince and a Saviour, and He only saves His people from their sins.

Other so-called saviours do but mock the hopes of mankind; they promise fairly, but they utterly deceive all who rely upon them. But this Holy Child, this blessed, glorious "God with us," has truly brought us salvation, and He saith, "Look unto Me, and be ye saved, all the ends of the earth: for I am God, and there is none else." This Jesus of Nazareth, the King of kings, and Lord of Lords, is the one and only Saviour. He, and none but He, shall save His people. He, and not another, shall save them by His own act and deed. Singly and unaided, He shall save His people. Personally, and not by another, in His own Name, and on His own behalf, He shall, by Himself, purge away His people's sins.

He shall do all the work, and leave none of it undone; He shall begin it, carry it on, and complete it; and therefore is His Name called Jesus, because He shall fully, entirely, and perfectly, save His people from their sins. The name Jesus has been, in a minor sense, applied to others aforetime; but now, henceforth, no one else may wear it, since there is no other Saviour but Christ the Lord; "neither is there salvation in any other: for there is none other name under Heaven given among men, whereby we must be saved."

VII. The Name of Jesus Indicates his Work

"Thou *shalt call His Name JESUS: for He shall save His people from their sins.*" He is not called Jesus because He is our Exemplar, though indeed He is perfection itself, and we long to tread in His footsteps; but He is called Jesus because He has come to seek and to save that which was lost.

He is Christ, too, or the Anointed, but then He is Christ *Jesus;* that is to say, it is as a Saviour that He is anointed. He is nothing at all if He is not a Saviour. He is anointed to this very end. His very Name is a sham if He does not save His people from their sins.

It is a gracious but very startling fact that our Lord's connection with His people lies in the direction of their sins. This is amazing condescension. He is called Saviour in connection with His people, but it is in reference to their sins, because it is from their sins that they need to be saved. If they had never sinned, they would never have required a Saviour, and there would have been no Name of Jesus known upon earth.

That is a wonderful text in Galatians 1:4, — did you ever meditate upon it? — "Who gave Himself for our sins, that He might deliver us from this present evil world, according to the will of God and our Father." It is true, as Martin Luther says, He never gave Himself for our righteousness, but He did give Himself for our sins. Sin is a horrible evil, a deadly poison, yet it is this which gives Jesus His title when He overcomes it. What a wonder this is! The first link between my soul and Christ is, not my goodness, but my badness; not my merit, but my misery; not my standing, but my falling; not my riches, but my need. He comes to visit His people, yet not to admire their beauties, but to remove their deformities; not to reward their virtues, but to forgive their sins.

O ye sinners,—I mean you real sinners,—not you who call yourselves by that name simply because you are told that is what you are, but you who really feel yourselves to be guilty before God, here is good news for you! O you self-condemned sinners, who feel that, if you are ever to get salvation, Jesus must bring it to you, and be the beginning and the end of it, I pray you to rejoice in this dear, this precious, this blessed Name, for Jesus has come to save you, even you! Go to Him as sinners, call Him "Jesus," and say to Him, "O Lord Jesus, be Jesus to me, save me, for I need Thy salvation!" Doubt not that He will fulfil His own Name, and exhibit His saving power in you. Only confess to Him your sin, and He will save you from it. Only believe in Him, and He will be your salvation.

What does Paul mean when he says "that Christ Jesus came into the world to save sinners"? He means, first, that Jesus came *to save them from the punishment of their sin.* Their sin shall not be laid to their charge, so that they shall be condemned for it, if they do but trust in Him who was punished in the place of those who were really guilty. That is one thing that Christ Jesus came into the world to do for sinners.

He came, also, *to save them from the pollution of their sin,* so that, though their mind has been debased, and their taste degraded, and their conscience deadened by sin, He came to take that evil away, and to give them a tender heart, and a hatred of sin, and a love for holiness, and a desire for purity. That is a great work for Him to accomplish, yet Jesus came to do even more than that.

He came, also, *to take away our tendencies to sin*, those tendencies which are born in us, and which grow up with us. He came by His Spirit to eradicate them, to pluck them up by the roots, and to put within us another principle, which shall fight with the old principle of sin, and overcome it, till Christ alone shall reign, and every thought shall be brought into captivity to Him.

Further, Jesus came *to save His people from apostasy*. He "came into the world to save sinners," in the fullest possible sense, by keeping them faithful to the end, so that they shall not go back unto perdition. This is a very important part of the work of Divine grace. To start a man right, is but little; but to keep that man holding on even to the end, is a triumph of almighty grace, and this is what Christ has come to do.

"Christ Jesus came into the world," not to half save you, not to save you in this, direction or that, and in this light or that, but to save you from your sin, to save you from an angry temper, to save you from pride, to save you from strong drink, to save you from covetousness, to save you from every evil thing, "and to present you faultless before the presence of His glory with exceeding joy." This is a glorious truth, "Christ Jesus came into the world to save sinners." He came to Bethlehem's manger, and afterwards to Calvary's cross, with this as His one business, that He might save sinners. Is He not able to save? Is He not just the Saviour that we need? God and yet man in one adorable Person, He is able to sympathize because He is man, and He is able to save because He is God. Blessed God-Man, Jesus Christ, Thou art able and willing to save me, and Thou art able and willing to save all other sinners who will believe in Thee!

VIII. Christ's Incarnation, At the Right Time

Paul wrote to the Galatians, "*When the fulness of the time was come,* God sent forth His Son, made of a woman, made under the law, to redeem them that were under the law, that we might receive the adoption of sons." The reservoir of time had to be filled by the inflowing of age after age; and when it was full to the brim, the Son of God appeared. Why the world should have remained without Him who is its one great Light for four thousand years after Adam was formed out of the dust of the earth, and why it should have taken that length of time for the Jewish Church to attain her full age, we cannot tell; but this we are plainly told, that Jesus was sent forth "when the fulness of the time was come." Our Lord did not come before His time, nor behind His time; He was punctual to the appointed hour, and cried, to the exact moment, "Lo, I come."

We may not curiously pry into the reasons why Christ came just when He did; but we may reverently muse on the great fact. The birth of Jesus is the grandest light of history, the sun in the heavens of all time. It is the pole-star of human destiny, the hinge of chronology, the meeting-place of the waters of the past and the future. Why did it happen just at that moment?

The main reason is, because it was so predicted. There were many prophecies, in the Old Testament Scriptures, which pointed, as with unerring fingers, to the place, the manner, and the time when the Shiloh would come, and the great sacrifice for sin should be offered. Jesus came at the very hour which God had determined.

The omniscient Lord of all appoints the date of every event; all times are in His hand, none are left to chance. There are no loose threads in the providence of God, and no dropped stitches. The great clock of the universe keeps perfect time, and the whole machinery of providence moves with unerring punctuality. It was to be expected that the greatest of all events should be most accurately and wisely timed, and so it was. God willed it to be when and where it was, and that will is to us the ultimate reason.

IX. CHRIST'S INCARNATION, A QUIETUS TO FEAR

THE angel said to the shepherds, "*Fear not:* for, behold, I bring you good tidings of great joy, which shall be to all people. For unto you is born this day in the city of David a Saviour, which is Christ the Lord." The very object for which He was born, and came into this world, was that He might deliver us from sin. What, then, was it that made us afraid? Were we not afraid of God, because we felt that we were lost through sin? Well, then, here is joy upon joy, for not only has the Lord come among us as a man, but He was made man in order that He might save man from that which separated him from God.

I feel as if the sorrow of my heart would flow forth in a flood of tears over the many sinners who have gone far away from God, and have been spending their lives riotously in various evil ways. I know they are afraid to come back; they think that the Lord will not receive them, and that there is no mercy for such sinners as they have been. But Jesus Christ has come to seek and to save that which was lost. If He does not save, He was born in vain, for the object of His birth was the salvation of sinners. If He shall not be a Saviour, then His mission in coming to this earth has missed its end, for its design was that lost sinners might be saved.

Lost one, lost one, if there were news that an angel had come to save thee, there might be some good cheer in it; but there are better tidings still. God Himself has come; the Infinite, the Almighty, has stooped from the highest heaven that He may pick thee up, a poor undone and worthless worm. Is there not comfort for thee here? Does not the Incarnation of the Saviour take away the horrible dread which hangs over men like a black pall?

The angel described the new-born Saviour as "*Christ*." There is His manhood, for it was as man that He was anointed. But the angel also rightly called Him "Christ *the Lord*." There is His God-head. This is the solid truth upon which we plant our foot. Jesus of Nazareth is "very God of very God." He who was born in Bethlehem's manger is now, and always was, "over all, God blessed for ever."

There is no Gospel at all if Christ be not God. It is no news to me to tell me that a great prophet is born. There have been great prophets before; but the world has never been redeemed from evil by mere testimony to the truth, and it never will be. But tell me that God is born, that God Himself has espoused our nature, and taken it into union with Himself, then the bells of my heart ring merry peals, for now may I come to God since God has come to me.

God has sent an Ambassador who inspires no fear. Not with helmet and coat of mail, not with sword or spear, does Heaven's Herald approach us; but the white flag is held in the hand of a Child, in the hand of One chosen out of the people, in the hand of One who died, in the hand of One who, though He reigns in glory, wears the nailprints still.

O man, God comes to you in the form of one like yourself! Do not be afraid to draw near to the gentle Jesus. Do not imagine that you need to be prepared for an audience with Him, or that you must have the intercession of a saint, or the intervention of priest or minister. Anyone could have come to the Babe in Bethlehem. The horned oxen, methinks, ate of the hay on which He slept, and feared not. It is the terror of the Godhead which, oftentimes, keeps the sinner away from reconciliation; but see how the Godhead is graciously concealed in that little Babe, who needed to be wrapped in swaddling-bands like any other new-born child. Who feareth to approach Him? Yet is the Godhead there.

My soul, when thou canst not, for very amazement, stand on the sea of glass mingled with fire, when the Divine glory is like a consuming fire to thy spirit, and the sacred majesty of Heaven is altogether overpowering to thee, then come thou to this Babe, and say, "Yet God is here, and here can I meet Him in the person of His dear Son, in whom dwelleth all the fulness of the Godhead bodily." Oh, what bliss there is in the Incarnation of Christ as we remember that therein God's omnipotence cometh down to man's feebleness, and infinite majesty stoops to man's infirmity!

The shepherds were not to find this Babe wrapped in Tyrian purple, nor swathed in choicest fabrics fetched from afar.

> "No crown bedecks His forehead fair,
>   No pearl, nor gem, nor silk is there."

Nor would they discover Him in the marble halls of princes, nor guarded by prætorian legionaries, nor attended by vassal sovereigns; but they would find Him the babe of a peasant woman, —of princely lineage, it is true, but of a family whose stock was dry and forgotten in Israel. The Holy Child was reputed to be the son of a carpenter. If you looked on the humble father and mother, and at the poor bed they had made up, where aforetime oxen had come to feed, you would say, "This is condescension indeed."

O ye poor, be glad, for Jesus is born in poverty, and cradled in a manger! O ye sons of toil, rejoice, for the Saviour is born of a lowly virgin, and a carpenter is His foster-father! O ye people, oftentimes

despised and downtrodden, the Prince of the de-
mocracy is born, One chosen out of the people is
exalted to the throne! O ye who call yourselves
the aristocracy, behold the Prince of the kings of
the earth, whose lineage is Divine, and yet there
is no room for Him in the inn! Behold, O men, the
Son of God, who is bone of your bone, and flesh of
your flesh; who, in His after life, was intimate with
all your griefs, hungered as ye hunger, was weary
as ye are weary, and wore humble garments like
your own; yea, suffered worse poverty than you
do, for He was without a place whereon to lay His
head! Let the heavens and the earth be glad, since
God hath so fully, so truly come down to man.

Jesus is the Friend of the poor, the sinful, and
the unworthy. You, poor ones, need not fear to
come unto Him; for He was born in a stable, and
cradled in a manger. You have not worse accommodation than He had; you are not poorer than
He was. Come and welcome to the poor man's
Prince, to the peasant's Saviour. Stay not back
through fear of your unfitness; the shepherds
came to Him in all their *déshabille*. I read not that
they tarried to put on their best garments; but, in
the clothes in which they wrapped themselves that
cold midnight, they hastened, just as they were, to
the young Child's presence. God looks not at garments, but at hearts; and accepts men when they
come to Him with willing spirits, whether they be
rich or poor.

X. Christ's Incarnation, Joyous and Personal

To the shepherds the angel said, "Behold, I bring you *good tidings of great joy*, which shall be to all people;" and, truly, the angelic message is still the source of joy to all who hear it aright: "*Unto you is born ... a Saviour*." Rejoice, then, ye who feel that ye are lost; for Christ Jesus the Saviour comes to seek and to save you. Be of good cheer, ye who are in the prison-house of sin, for He comes to set you free. Ye who are famished and ready to die, rejoice that Christ Jesus the Lord has consecrated for you a better Bethlehem, a true "house of bread," and that He has Himself come to be the bread of life to your souls. Rejoice, O sinners, everywhere, for the Restorer of the castaways, the Saviour of the fallen, is born!

Join in the joy, ye saints, for He is also the Preserver of the saved ones, delivering them from innumerable perils, and He is the sure Perfecter of all whom He preserves. Jesus is no partial Saviour, beginning a work, and never completing it; but, saving and cleansing, restoring and upholding, He also perfects and presents the saved ones, without spot, or wrinkle, or any such thing, before His Father's face. Rejoice, then, all ye people; let your hills and valleys ring with joy, for a Saviour, who is mighty to save, is born among you.

This joy began with the shepherds, for the angel said to them, "Unto *you* is born this day in the city of David a Saviour, which is Christ the Lord." Reader, shall the joy begin with you to-day? It avails you little that Christ is born, or that Christ died, unless unto *you* a Child is born, and for *you* Jesus bled. A personal interest in the birth, life, and death of Christ is the main point for each one of us.

"But I am poor," saith one. So were the shepherds. O ye poor, to you this mysterious Child is born! "The poor have the Gospel preached unto them." "He shall judge the poor of the people, He shall save the children of the needy, and shall break in pieces the oppressor."

"But I am obscure and unknown," saith one. So were the watchers on the midnight plain. Who, save God, knew the men who endured hard toil, and kept their flocks by night? And you, unknown of men, are known to God; shall it not, then, be said that "unto you a Child is born"? The Lord regardeth not the greatness of men, but He hath respect unto the lowly.

Possibly, you say that you are illiterate, you cannot understand much. Be it so; but unto the shepherds Christ was born, and their simplicity did not hinder them from receiving Him, but even helped them to do so. Let it be so with yourself; receive gladly the simple truth as it is in Jesus. The Lord hath exalted One chosen out of the people.

No aristocratic Christ have I to commend to you, but the Saviour of the people, the Friend of publicans and sinners. Jesus is the true "poor man's Friend;" He is "a Witness to the people, a Leader and Commander to the people." Oh, that each one of us might truly say, "Unto me is Jesus born"! If I truly believe in Him, Christ is born unto me, and I may be as sure of it as if an angel announced it personally to me, since the Scripture assures me that, if I believe in Jesus, He is mine, and I am His, and through union with Him I become a partaker in His everlasting life, and in all that He has.

XI. Christ's Incarnation, The Wonder of Angels

How surprised the angels must have been when they were first informed that Jesus Christ, the Prince of life, intended to shroud Himself in clay, and become a human babe, and live and die upon the earth! We know not how the information was first communicated to the angels; but when the rumour began to circulate among the shining hosts, we may imagine what strange wonderment there was in their lofty minds. What! was it true that He, whose crown was all bedight with stars, would lay that crown aside? What! was it certain that He, about whose shoulders was cast the purple robe of universal sovereignty, would become a man, dressed in a peasant's garment? Could it be true that He, who was everlasting and immortal, would one day be nailed to a cross? How their wonderment must have increased as the details of the Saviour's life and death were made known to them. Well might they desire to "look into" these things, which were so surprising and mysterious to them.

And when He descended from on high, they followed Him; for Jesus was "seen of angels," and seen in a very special sense; for they looked upon Him in rapturous amazement, wondering what it could mean when He, "who was rich, for our sakes became poor." Do you see Him as, on that day of Heaven's eclipse, He did, as it were, ungird Himself of His majesty? Can you conceive the increasing wonder of the heavenly hosts when the great deed was actually done, when they saw His priceless tiara taken off, when they watched Him unbind His girdle of stars, and cast away His sandals of gold? Can you conceive what must have been the astonishment of the angels when He said to them, "I do not disdain the womb of the virgin; I am going down to earth to become a man"? Can you picture them as they declared that they would follow Him? They followed Him as near as He would permit them; and when they came to earth, they began to sing, "Glory to God in the highest, and on earth peace, good will toward men." Nor would they go away till they had made the shepherds also wonder, and till heaven had hung out new stars in honour of the new-born King.

And now wonder, ye angels, as ye see that the Infinite has become an infant. He, upon whose shoulders the universe doth hang, hangs at His mother's breast. He, who created all things by the word of His power, and who bears up the pillars of creation, hath now become so weak that He must be carried in the arms of a woman! Wonder, ye that knew Him in His riches, whilst ye behold Him in His poverty. Where sleeps the new-born King? Hath He the best room in Cæsar's palace? Hath a cradle of gold been prepared for Him, and pillows of down, on which to rest His head? No; in the dilapidated stable where the oxen stood, and in the manger where they fed, there the Saviour lies, swathed in the swaddling-bands of the children of poverty. Nor doth He rest long there; on a sudden, His mother must carry Him to Egypt; He must go there, and become a stranger in a strange land. When He came back, and grew up at Nazareth, the angels must have marvelled to see Him that made the worlds handle the hammer and the nails, assisting His reputed father in the trade of a carpenter.

XII. Christ's Incarnation, The Marvel of Mortals

If the angels were so astonished at Christ's birth, it is not surprising that man should be filled with holy wonder at the great mystery. That God should have such consideration for His fallen creatures that, instead of sweeping them away with the besom of destruction, He should devise a wonderful scheme for their redemption, and that He should Himself undertake to be their Redeemer, and to pay their ransom price, is, indeed, marvellous.

Probably, it will seem most marvellous to you in its relation to yourself, that *you* should be redeemed by the precious blood of Jesus, that God should forsake the thrones and royalties above to suffer ignominiously below for *you*. If you truly know yourself, you can never see any adequate motive or reason in your own self for such a wonderful deed as this. "Why should God display such love to me?" you may well ask.

If David, when the Lord revealed to him the honours in store for him and for his family, could only say, "Who am I, O Lord God, and what is my house, that Thou hast brought me hitherto? And is this the manner of man, O Lord God?" what should you and I say? Had we been the most meritorious of individuals, and had we unceasingly kept the Lord's commands, we could not have deserved such a priceless boon as Christ's Incarnation; but as we are sinners, offenders, rebels, who have revolted, and continually gone further and further away from God, what shall we say of this incarnate God dying for us, but "Herein is love, not that we loved God, but that He loved us, and sent His Son to be the propitiation for our sins"?

Let your soul lose itself in wonder, for wonder is, in this way, a very practical emotion. Holy wonder will lead you to *grateful worship;* being amazed at what God has done, you will pour out your soul with astonishment at the foot of the golden throne in the grateful and adoring song, "Blessing, and honour, and glory, and majesty, and power, and dominion, and might be unto Him who sitteth on the throne, and doeth these great things to me."

This wonder will also produce in you *godly watchfulness;* you will be afraid to sin against such love as this. Feeling the presence of the mighty God in the gift of His dear Son, you will put off your shoes from off your feet, because the place whereon you stand is holy ground.

You will be moved, at the same time, to *a glorious hope.* If Jesus has given Himself to you, if He has done this marvellous thing on your behalf, you will feel that Heaven itself is not too great for your expectation, and that the rivers of pleasure at God's right hand are not too sweet or too deep for you to drink thereof. Who can be astonished at anything when he has once learned the mystery of the manger and the cross?

What is there wonderful left after one has seen the Saviour? The nine wonders of the world! Why, you may put them all into a nutshell,—machinery and modern art can excel them all; but this one wonder is not the wonder of earth only, but of Heaven and earth, and even of hell itself. It is not the wonder of the olden time, but the wonder of all time, and the wonder of eternity. They who see human wonders a few times, at last cease to be astonished; the noblest pile that architect ever raised, at last fails to impress the onlooker; but not so this marvellous temple of incarnate Deity; the more we look at it, the more we are astonished;

the more we become accustomed to it, the more have we a sense of its surpassing splendour of love and grace. There is more of God's glory and majesty to be seen in the manger and the cross, than in the sparkling stars above, the rolling deep below, the towering mountain, the teeming valleys, the abodes of life, or the abyss of death. Let us then give ourselves up to holy wonder, such as will produce gratitude, worship, love, and confidence, as we think of that great "mystery of godliness, God manifest in the flesh."

XIII. Emmanuel, "God with Us"

In addition to explaining the Name of Jesus, and recording its God-given origin, the Holy Spirit, by the evangelist Matthew, has been pleased to refer us to the synonym of it, and so to give us still more of its meaning. "Now all this was done, that it might be fulfilled which was spoken of the Lord by the prophet, saying, Behold, a virgin shall be with child, and shall bring forth a Son, and they shall call His Name Emmanuel, which being interpreted is, God with us." If, when our Lord was born, and named "Jesus," the old prophecy which said that He should be called Emmanuel was fulfilled, it follows that the name "Jesus" bears a signification tantamount to that of "Emmanuel," and that its virtual meaning is "God with us." And, indeed, He is Jesus, the Saviour, because He is Emmanuel, God with us; and as soon as He was born, and so became Emmanuel, the incarnate God, He became by that very fact Jesus, the Saviour. By coming down from Heaven to this earth, and taking upon Himself our nature, He bridged the otherwise bridgeless gulf between God and man; by suffering in that human nature, and imparting, through His Divine nature, an infinite efficacy to His suffering, He removed that which would have destroyed us, and brought us everlasting life and salvation. O Jesus, dearest of all names in earth or in Heaven, I love thy music all the better because it is in such sweet harmony with another Name which rings melodiously in mine ears, — Emmanuel, God with us!

Our Saviour is *God*, and therefore He is

"mighty to save;" He is God *with us*, and therefore
pitiful; He is Divine, and therefore infinitely wise;
but He is human, and therefore full of compassion.
Never let us for a moment hesitate as to the Godhead of our Lord Jesus Christ, for His Deity is a
fundamental doctrine of the Christian faith. It may
be that we shall never fully understand how God
and man could be united in one Person, for who
by searching can find out God? These great mysteries of godliness, these "deep things of God," are
beyond our measurement. Our little skiff might be
lost if we ventured so far out upon this vast, this
infinite ocean, as to lose sight of the shore of plain-
ly-revealed truth.

But let it remain, as a matter of faith, that Jesus
Christ, even He who lay in Bethlehem's manger,
and was carried in a woman's arms, and lived a
suffering life, and died on a malefactor's cross,
was, nevertheless, the appointed "Heir of all
things," the brightness of His Father's glory, "and
the express image of His person," "who thought
it not a prize to be grasped to be equal with God,"
for that honour was already His, so that He could
truly say, "I and My Father are one."

Jesus of Nazareth was certainly not an angel. That fact the apostle Paul has abundantly
disproved in the first and second chapters of his
Epistle to the Hebrews. He could not have been an
angel, for honours are ascribed to Him which were
never bestowed on angels. He was no subordinate
deity, or created being elevated to the Godhead, as
some have absurdly said. All such statements are
as unreliable as dreams and falsehoods. Christ was
as surely God as He could be, one with the Father
and the ever-blessed Spirit. If it were not so, not
only would the great strength of our hope be gone,
but the glory of the Incarnation would have evap-
orated altogether. The very essence of it is that it
was God Himself who was veiled in human flesh;
if it was any other being who thus came to us, I see

nothing very remarkable in it, nothing comforting, certainly. That an angel should become a man, is a matter of no great consequence to me; that some other superior being should assume the nature of man, brings no joy to my heart, and opens no well of consolation to me.

But "God with us" is the source of exquisite delight. "God with us" — all that "God" means, the Deity, the infinite Jehovah with us, — this, this is worthy of the burst of midnight song, when angels startled the shepherds with their carols, singing "Glory to God in the highest, and on earth peace, good will toward men." This was worthy of the foresight of seers and prophets, worthy of a new star in the heavens, worthy of the care which Inspiration has manifested to preserve the record.

This, too, was worthy of the martyr-deaths of apostles and confessors, who counted not their lives dear unto them for the sake of the incarnate God; and this is worthy, at this day, of our most earnest endeavours to spread the glad tidings, worthy of a holy life to illustrate its blessed influences, and worthy of a joyful death to prove its consoling power. Well did the apostle say, "Without controversy great is the mystery of godliness: God was manifest in the flesh." He who was born at Bethlehem is God, and "God with us." God — there lies the majesty; "God with us," there lies the mercy. God — therein is glory; "God *with us*," therein is grace. God alone might well strike us with terror; but "God with us" inspires us with hope and confidence.

XIV. "GOD WITH US,"
UNPARALLELED CONDESCENSION

THIS gracious Emmanuel—"God with us"—was the great Creator. "All things were made by Him; and without Him was not any thing made that was made." He reigned in Heaven as the acknowledged equal with the Father. The angels delighted to do Him homage; every seraph's wing would fly at His bidding; all the host of Heaven worshipped at His feet. Hymned day without night by all the sacred choristers, He did not lack for praise. Nor did He lack for servants; legions of angels were ever ready to do His commandments, hearkening unto the voice of His word.

All the powers of nature, too, were under His control. He wanted nothing to make Him glorious; all things were His, and the power to make more if He needed them. He could truly say, "If I were hungry, I would not tell thee: for the world is Mine, and the fulness thereof." It was this God, this Ever-blessed One, who had been from eternity with the Father, and in whom the Father had infinite delight, who looked upon men with the eye of love. He that was born in Bethlehem's manger, He that lived here the life of a peasant, toiling and suffering, was one with Jehovah.

Well might Isaiah, in his prophetic vision, proclaim the royal titles of the "Child" who was to be born, and the "Son" who, in the fulness of time, would be given to us and for us: "The government shall be upon His shoulder: and His Name shall be called Wonderful, Counsellor, The Mighty

God, The everlasting Father, The Prince of Peace."
Let this truth sink into our souls, that it was God
Himself who came from Heaven to save us from
destruction. It was no inferior being, no one like
ourselves; but it was "very God of very God" who
loved us with an everlasting and infinite affection.
I have often turned that thought over in my mind,
but I have never been able to express it as I have
wished.

If I were told that all the sons of men cared for
me, that would be but as a drop in a bucket compared with Jehovah Himself regarding me with favour. If it were said that all the princes of the earth
had fallen at some poor man's feet, and laid aside
their dignities that they might relieve his necessi-
ties, it would be counted condescending kindness;
but such an act would not be worthy to be spoken
of in comparison with that infinite condescension
and unparalleled love which brought the Saviour
from the skies to rescue and redeem such worthless rebels as we were. It is not possible that all the
condescension of all the kind and compassionate
men who have ever lived should be more than as
a small grain that could not turn the scale, compared with the everlasting hills of the Saviour's
wondrous love.

What amazing condescension is it that God,
who made all things, should assume the nature
of one of His own creatures, that the Self-existent
should be united with the dependent and derived,
and the Almighty linked with the feeble and
mortal! In His Incarnation, our Lord Jesus Christ
descended to the very depths of humiliation, by
entering into alliance with a nature which did not
occupy the chief place in the scale of existence.
It would have been marvellous condescension
for the infinite and incomprehensible Jehovah to
have taken upon Himself the nature of some noble spiritual being, such as a seraph or a cherub.
The union of the Divine Creator with any created

spirit would have been an immeasurable stoop;
but for God to become one with man, is far greater
condescension.

Remember that, in the person of Christ, manhood was not merely an immortal spirit, but also
suffering, hungering, dying, flesh and blood.
There was taken to Himself, by our Lord, all that
materialism which makes up a human body; and
that body is, after all, formed out of the dust of
the earth, a structure fashioned from the materials
which lie all around us. There is nothing in our
bodily frame but what is to be found in the substance of the earth on which we live. We feed upon
that which groweth out of the earth; and when we
die, we go back to the dust from whence we were
taken. Is it not a strange thing that this grosser part
of creation, this meaner part, this dust of it, should
nevertheless be taken into union with that pure, incomprehensible Divine Being, of whom we know
so little, and of whom we can really comprehend
nothing at all? Oh, the condescension of it! I must
leave it to the meditations of your quiet moments.
Dwell on it with awe. I am persuaded that no man
has any adequate idea how wonderful a stoop it
was for God thus to dwell in human flesh, and to
be "God with us."

Yet, to realize in it something that is still more
remarkable, remember that the creature whose
nature Christ took was a being who had sinned
against Him. I can more readily conceive of the
Lord taking upon Himself the nature of a race
which had never fallen; but, lo! man stood in rebellion against God, and yet a man did Christ become,
that He might deliver us from the consequences of
our rebellion, and lift us up to something higher
than our pristine purity. "Oh, the depths!" is all
that we can say, as we look on and marvel at this
stoop of Divine love.

XV. "GOD WITH US," THE MYSTERY OF MYSTERIES

IT must ever remain to us the mystery of mysteries that God Himself was manifest in the flesh. God the invisible was manifest; God the spiritual dwelt in mortal flesh; God the infinite, uncontained, boundless, was manifest in the flesh. What infinite leagues our thought must traverse between God-head self-existent, and, therefore, full of power and self-sufficiency, before we have descended to the far-down level of poor human flesh, which is, at its best, but as grass, and, in its essence, only so much animated dust! Where can we find a greater contrast than between God and flesh?

Yet the two are perfectly blended in the Incarnation of Jesus Christ the Saviour of the lost. "God was manifest in the flesh;" truly God, not God humanised, but God as God. He was manifest in real flesh; not in manhood deified, and made superhuman, but in actual flesh.

Since this matchless truth is "without controversy," let us not enter into any controversy about it, but let us reverently meditate upon it. What *a miracle of condescension* is here, that God should manifest Himself in flesh! This is not so much a theme for the tongue or the pen, as something that is to be pondered in the heart. It needs that we sit down in quietness, and consider how He, who made us, became like us; how He, who is our God, became our Brother-Man; how He, who is adored of angels, once lay in a manger; how He, who feeds all living things, hungered and was

athirst; how He, who oversees all worlds as God,
was, as a man, made to sleep, to suffer, and to die
like ourselves. This is a statement not easily to be
believed. If He had not been beheld by many wit-
nesses, so that men handled Him, looked upon
Him, and heard Him speak, it would have been a
matter not readily to be accepted that so Divine a
Person should ever have been manifest in flesh. It
is a wonder of condescension.

And it is, also, *a marvel of benediction*, for God's
manifestation in human flesh conveys a thousand
blessings to us. Bethlehem's star is the morning
star of hope to believers. Now, man is nearest to
God of all His creatures; now, between poor puny
man that is born of a woman, and the infinite God,
there is a bond of union of the most wonderful
kind. The Lord Jesus Christ is God and man in
one Person. This brings our manhood very near
to God, and by so doing it ennobles our nature, it
lifts us up from the dunghill, and sets us among
princes; while, at the same time, it enriches us
by endowing our manhood with all the glory of
Christ Jesus, in whom dwelleth all the fulness of
the Godhead bodily.

Lift up your eyes, ye down-trodden sons of
men, for ye have a brotherhood with Christ, and
Christ is God. O ye, who have begun to despise
yourselves, and think that ye are merely sent to
be drudges upon earth, and slaves of sin, lift up
your heads, and look for redemption to the Son of
man, who has broken the captives' bonds! If ye be
believers in the Christ of God, then are ye also the
children of God; "and if children, then heirs; heirs
of God, and joint-heirs with Christ."

There is, in this truth, *a fulness of consolation*,
as well as of condescension and benediction; for
if the Son of God be man, then He understands
me, and He has a fellow-feeling for me. He knows,
at times, my unfitness even to worship Him; He
knows my tendencies to grow weary and cold in

His service; He knows my pains, my trials, and my griefs; yea, —

> "He knows what fierce temptations mean,
>   For He has felt the same."

Man, truly man, yet sitting at the right hand of the Father, Thou, O blessed Saviour, art the delight of my soul! Is there not the richest comfort in this truth for all the people of God?

And, withal, there is *most gracious instruction*, too, for God was manifest in the flesh. If we desire to see God, we must see Him in Christ Jesus. The apostle does not say that God was veiled in the flesh, though under certain aspects that might be true; but he says that "God was *manifest* in the flesh." The brightness of the sun might put out our eyes if we gazed upon it, and we must needs look through dim glass, and then the sun is manifested to us; so, the excessive glory of the infinite Godhead cannot be borne by our mind's eye till it comes into communication and union with the nature of man, and then God is manifest to us.

My soul, never try to gaze upon an absolute God; the brightness of the Deity will blind thine eye, "for our God is a consuming fire." Ask not to see God in fire in the burning bush, nor in the lightning upon Mount Sinai; be satisfied to see Him in the man Christ Jesus, for there God is manifested. Not all the glory of the sky and of the sea, nor the wonders of Creation and Providence, can set forth the Deity as does the Son of Mary, who from the manger went to the cross, and from the cross to the tomb, and from the tomb to His eternal throne at His Father's right hand in glory.

That "God was manifest in the flesh," is one of the most extraordinary doctrines that was ever declared in human hearing. Were it not so well attested, it would be absolutely incredible that the infinite God, who filleth all things, who was, and is, and is to come, the Omnipotent, the Omniscient, and the Omnipresent, actually condescended to veil Himself in the garments of our inferior clay. He made us, yet He deigned to take the flesh of His creatures into union with Himself; the Eternal was blended with mortality. That manger at Bethlehem, tenanted by the express image of the Father's glory, was a great sight indeed to those who understood it. Well might the angels troop forth in crowds from within the gates of pearl, that they might behold Him, whom Heaven could not contain, finding accommodation in a stable with a lowly wedded pair. Wonder of wonders! Marvel of marvels! Mystery of mysteries!

The greatness of this mystery consists, first, in the fact that *it concerns God*. Any doctrine which relates to the Infinite and the Eternal is of the utmost importance to us. We should be all ear and all heart when we have to learn anything concerning God. Reason teaches us that He who made us, who is our Preserver, and at whose word we are so soon to return to the dust, should be the first object of our thoughts. Turn ye hither, ye wayward children of Adam, and behold this great mystery, for your God is here.

The mystery of God "manifest in the flesh" will also appear to you great if you consider *the great honour which is thereby conferred upon manhood*. How wonderfully is mankind honoured in God's taking the nature of man into union with Himself! "For verily He took not on Him the nature of angels; but He took on Him the seed of Abraham." Whichever of all His creatures shall come nearest to the Creator will evidently have the pre-eminence in the ranks of creatureship; which, then, shall bear the palm? Shall not the seraphs be the chosen ones? Shall not the swift-winged sons of light be chief among Heaven's courtiers? Behold, and be astonished, a worm of earth is preferred to the angels; rebellious man is chosen, and the sinless angels are passed over! Human nature is espoused into oneness with the Divine!

There is, at this hour, no gulf between God and redeemed man. God is first, but next comes man in the person of the God-Man, Christ Jesus. Well may we say, with David, "When I consider Thy heavens, the work of Thy fingers, the moon and the stars, which Thou hast ordained; what is man, that Thou art mindful of him? and the son of man, that Thou visitest him? For Thou hast made him a little lower than the angels, and hast crowned him with glory and honour. Thou madest him to have dominion over the works of Thy hands; Thou hast put all things under his feet." Man became royal when Christ became human. Man was exalted when Christ was humiliated. Man may go up to God now that God has come down to man. This is a great mystery, is it not? A mystery, certainly, but great in every way. See that ye despise it not, lest ye miss the abounding benefit which flows to man through this golden channel.

XVI. "God With Us," Bridging The Great Gulf

The Eternal seems to be so far away from us. He is infinite, and we are such little creatures. There appears to be a great gulf fixed between man and God, even in the matter of our creatureship. But He, who is God, has also become man. We never heard that God took the nature of angels into union with Himself; we may therefore say that, between Godhead and angelhood, there must be an infinite distance still; but the Lord has actually taken manhood into union with Himself. There is, therefore, no longer a great gulf between Him and us. On the contrary, here is a marvellous union; Godhead has entered into marriage bonds with manhood.

O my soul, thou dost not stand now, like a poor lone orphan, wailing across the deep sea after thy Father, who has gone far away, and cannot hear thee; thou dost not now sob and sigh, like an infant left naked and helpless, its Maker having gone too far away to supply its wants, or listen to its cries! No, thy Maker has become like thyself. Is that too strong a word to use? He, without whom was not anything made that was made, was made flesh; and He was made flesh in such a way that He was tempted in all points like as we are, yet without sin. O manhood, was there ever such good news as this for thee? Poor manhood, thou weak worm of the dust, far lower than the angels, lift up thy head, and be not afraid! Poor manhood, born in weakness, living in toil, covered with sweat, and dying at last to be eaten by the worms, be not thou abashed even in the presence of seraphs, for next to God is man, and not even an archangel can come in between; nay, not merely next to God, for Jesus, who is God, is man also; Jesus Christ, eternally God, was born, and lived, and died as we also do.

Our Lord Jesus Christ is, in some senses, more completely man than Adam ever was. Adam was not born; he was created as a man. Adam never had to struggle through the risks and weaknesses of infancy; he knew not the littlenesses of child-hood,—he was full-grown at once. Father Adam could not sympathize with me as a babe and a child. But how manlike is Jesus! He does not begin with us in mid-life, as Adam did; but He is cradled with us, He accompanies us in the pains, and fee-bleness, and infirmities of infancy, and He contin-ues with us even to the grave.

There is sweet comfort in the thought that He who is this day God, was once an infant; so that, if my cares are little, and even trivial and compar-atively infantile, I may go to Him with them, for He was once a child. Though the great ones of the earth may sneer at the child of poverty, and say, "You are too mean for us to notice, and your trou-ble is too slight to evoke our pity;" I recollect, with humble joy, that the King of Heaven was wrapped in swaddling-bands, and carried in a woman's arms; and therefore I may tell Him all my griefs. How wonderful that He should have been an in-fant, and yet should be God, blessed for ever! The Holy Child Jesus bridges the great gulf between me and God.

There was never a subject of sweeter song than this,—the stooping down of Godhead to the fee-bleness of manhood. When God manifested His power in the works of His hands, the morning stars sang together, and the sons of God shout-ed for joy; but when God manifests *Himself*, what

music shall suffice for the grand psalm of adoring
wonder? When wisdom and power are seen, these
are but attributes of Deity; but in the Incarnation
of Christ, it is the Divine Person Himself who is revealed, though He is, in a measure, hidden in our
inferior clay. Well might Mary sing, when earth
and Heaven even now are wondering at the condescending grace by which "the Word was made
flesh, and dwelt among us."

We can never think that God sits on high, in-
different to the wants and woes of men; for He has
visited us in our low estate. No longer need we
lament that we can never participate in the moral
glory and purity of God, for if God in glory can
come down to His sinful creature, it is certainly
less difficult for Him to bear that creature, blood-
washed and purified, up the starry way, that the
redeemed one may sit down for ever with Him on
His throne. Let us dream no longer, in sombre sad-
ness, that we cannot draw near to God, so that He
can really hear our prayers, and relieve our neces-
sities, for Jesus has become bone of our bone, and
flesh of our flesh, and, bowing His head to death
for us, He has opened that new and living way,
by which we may come with boldness, and have
access to the throne of the heavenly grace.

Angels sang the story of Christ's birth; yet, perhaps, they scarcely knew why they did so. Could
they understand why God had become man? They
must have known that herein was a great mystery
of condescension; but all the loving consequences
which the Incarnation involved, even their acute
minds could hardly have guessed; but *we* see the
whole, and comprehend the grand design most
fully. The manger of Bethlehem was big with glory; in Christ's Incarnation was wrapped up all the
blessedness by which a soul, snatched from the
depths of sin, is lifted up to the heights of glory.
Shall not our clearer knowledge lead us to heights
of song which angelic guesses could not reach?

Shall the lips of cherubs move to flaming sonnets, and shall we, who are redeemed by the blood of the incarnate God, be treacherously and ungratefully silent?

> "Did archangels sing Thy coming?
>   Did the shepherds learn their lays?
> Shame would cover me ungrateful,
>   Should my tongue refuse to praise."

XVII. "God with Us" Under All Conditions

Being "with us" in our nature, God is "with us" *in all our life's pilgrimage.* Scarcely can we find a single halting-place, in the march of life, at which Jesus has not paused, or a weary league of the road which He has not traversed. From the gate of entrance, even to the door which closes life's pilgrim way, the footprints of Jesus may be traced. Were you once in the cradle? He was there. Were you a child under parental authority? Christ also was a boy in the home at Nazareth. Have you entered upon life's battle? Your Lord and Master did the same; and though He lived not literally a long life, yet, through incessant toil and suffering, He bore the marred visage which usually attends a battered old age. He was not much more than thirty when the Jews said to Him, "Thou art not yet fifty years old," evidently implying that He looked much older than He actually was.

Are you alone? So was He, in the wilderness, and on the mountain's side, and in the garden's gloom. Do you mix in public society? So did He labour in the thickest press. Where can you find yourself, on the hill-top, or in the valley, on the land or on the sea, in the daylight or in darkness, without discovering that Jesus has been there before you? We might truly say of our Redeemer that He was—

> "A man so various that He seemed to be
> Not one, but all mankind's epitome."

One harmonious man He was, and yet all saintly lives seem to be condensed in His. Two believers may be very unlike each other, and yet both will find that Christ's life has in it points of resemblance to their own. One may be rich and another poor, one actively laborious and another patiently suffering, yet each man, in studying the history of the Saviour, shall be able to say, "His pathway ran hard by my own." He was in all points made like unto His brethren. How charming is the fact that our Lord is "God with us," not merely here and there, and now and then, but everywhere, and evermore!

Especially do we realize the sweetness of His being "God with us" *in our sorrows*. There is no pang that rends the heart, I might almost say not one which disturbs the body, but Jesus Christ has endured it before us. Do you feel the pinching of poverty? He could say, "The Son of man hath not where to lay His head." Do you know the grief of bereavement? "Jesus wept" at the tomb of Lazarus. Have you been slandered for righteousness' sake, and has it vexed your spirit? He said, "Reproach hath broken Mine heart." Have you been betrayed? Do not forget that He, too, had His familiar friend, who sold Him for the price of a slave. On what stormy seas have you been tossed which have not also roared around His boat? Never will you traverse any glen of adversity so dark, so dismal, apparently so pathless, but what, in stooping down, you may discover the footprints of the Crucified One. In the fires and in the rivers, in the cold night and under the burning sun, He cries, "I am with thee. Be not dismayed, for I am both thy Companion and thy God."

Mysteriously true is it that, when you and I shall come to *the last, the closing scene*, we shall find that Emmanuel has been there also. He felt the pangs and throes of death, He endured the bloody sweat of agony, and the parching thirst of fever.

He knew all about the separation of the tortured spirit from the poor fainting flesh, and cried, as we shall, "Father, into Thy hands I commend My spirit."

Ay, and He knew the grave, too, for there He slept, and left the sepulchre perfumed and furnished for us as a couch of rest, and not as a charnel-house of corruption. That new tomb in the garden makes Him "God with us" till the resurrection shall call us from our beds of clay to find Him "God with us" in newness of life. We shall be raised up in His likeness, and the first sight our opening eyes shall see will be our incarnate God. Every true believer can say, with Job, "I know that my Redeemer liveth, and that He shall stand at the latter day upon the earth: and though after my skin worms destroy this body, yet in my flesh shall I see God." Yes; I, in my flesh, shall see Him as the man, the God, the God-Man, Christ Jesus.

And *to all eternity* He will maintain the most intimate association with us. As long as the eternal ages roll, He will still be "God with us." Has He not said, "Because I live, ye shall live also"? Both His human and His Divine life will last for ever, and so shall our life endure. He shall dwell among us, and lead us to living fountains of waters, and so shall we be "for ever with the Lord."

Ask yourselves whether you know what "God with us" means. Has it been God with you in your tribulations, by the Holy Ghost's comforting influence? Has it been God with you in searching the Scriptures? Has the Holy Spirit shone upon the Word? Has it been God with you in conviction, bringing you to Sinai? Has it been God with you in comforting you, by bringing you to Calvary? Do you know the full meaning of that Name Emmanuel, "God with us"? No; he who knows it best knows but little of it; and, alas! he who knows it not at all is ignorant indeed; so ignorant that his ignorance is not bliss, but will be his damnation unless it is removed by the Holy Spirit's effectual working. May He teach you the meaning of that Name!

My soul, try to ring out the music of these words, "God with us." Put me in the desert, where vegetation grows not; I can still say, "God with us." Put me on the wild ocean, and let my ship dance madly on the waves; I would still say, "God with us." Mount me on the sunbeam, and let me fly beyond the Western sea; still I would say, "God with us." Let my body dive down into the depths of the ocean, and let me hide in its caverns; still I could, as a child of God, say, "God with us."

This is one of the bells of Heaven, let us strike it yet again: "God with us." It is a stray note from the sonnets of paradise: "God with us." It is the melody of the seraphs' song: "God with us." It is one of the notes of Jehovah Himself, when He rejoices over His Church with singing: "God with us."

Tell it out to all the nations that this is the Name of Him who was born in Bethlehem, "God with us,"—God with us, by His Incarnation, for the august Creator of the world did walk upon this globe; He, who made ten thousand orbs, each of them more mighty and more vast than this earth, became the inhabitant of this tiny atom. He, who was from everlasting to everlasting, came to this world of time, and stood upon the narrow neck of land betwixt the two unbounded seas.

His Name is, indeed, wonderful: "Emmanuel." It is wisdom's mystery: "God with us." Sages think of it, and wonder; angels desire to look into it; the plumb-line of reason cannot reach half-way into its depths; the eagle-wing of science cannot fly so high, and the piercing eye of the vulture of research cannot see it. "God with us." It is hell's terror. Satan trembles at the sound of it; his legions fly apace, the black-winged dragon of the pit quails before it. Let him come to attack you, and do you but whisper that word "Emmanuel," back he falls, confounded and confused. Satan trembles when he hears that Name, "Emmanuel." It is the Christian labourer's strength; how could he preach the Gospel, how could he bend his knees in prayer, how could the missionary go into foreign lands, how could the martyr stand at the stake, how could the confessor own his Master, how could men labour if that one word were taken away? "Emmanuel." 'Tis the sufferer's comfort, 'tis the balm for his woe, 'tis the alleviation of his misery, 'tis the sleep which God giveth to His beloved, 'tis their rest after exertion and toil. Ah! and more than that; 'tis eternity's sonnet, 'tis Heaven's hallelujah, 'tis the shout of the glorified, 'tis the song of the redeemed, 'tis the chorus of angels, 'tis the everlasting oratorio of the grand orchestra of the sky.

"Hail, great Emmanuel, all Divine,
   In Thee Thy Father's glories shine;
   Thou brightest, sweetest, fairest one,
   That eyes have seen, or angels known."

XVIII. THE GOD-MAN, CHRIST JESUS

IT was a new and startling doctrine, when first preached to heathen sages, that God would take humanity into so intimate a connection with Himself as really and truly to be man and God in the same person; but it is a doctrine which must be received by you, or else you cannot receive Christ.

My Master will not be satisfied with the acknowledgment that His character is lovely, His doctrine pure, and His moral teaching super-excellent. He will not be content with your admission that He is a Prophet greater than any prophet who ever came before or after Him. He will not rest satisfied with your admission that He is a Teacher sent from Heaven, and a being who, on account of His virtues, is now peculiarly exalted in Heaven.

All this is true, but it is not the whole truth; you must also believe that He who, as man, was born of the Virgin, and was dandled upon her lap at Bethlehem, was, as God, none other than the everlasting Lord, without beginning of days or end of years. You do not receive Christ in very deed and truth unless you believe in His real humanity and actual Godhead.

Indeed, what is there for you to receive if you do not receive this truth? A saviour who is not Divine can be no Saviour for us. How can a mere man, however eminent, deliver his fellows from sins such as yours and mine? How can he bear the burden of our guilt any more than we can ourselves bear it, if there be nothing more in him than

in any other singularly virtuous man? An angel
would stagger beneath the load of human crimi-
nality, and much more would this be the case with
even a perfect man, if such an one could be found.
It needed those mighty shoulders—

"Which bear the earth's huge pillars up,"—

to sustain the weight of human sin, and carry it
into the wilderness of forgetfulness. So, in order to
be saved by Him, you must receive Christ as being
God as well as man.

John calls Him "The Word," or the speech of
God. God in nature has revealed Himself, as it
were, inarticulately and indistinctly; but, in His
Son, He has revealed Himself as a man declares
his inmost thoughts, by distinct and intelligible
speech. Jesus is to the Father what speech is to
us; He is the unfolding of the Father's thoughts,
the revelation of the Father's heart. He that hath
seen Christ hath seen the Father. "Wouldst thou
have me see thee?" said Socrates, "then speak;" for
speech reveals the man. Wouldst thou see God?
Listen to Christ, for He is God's Word, revealing
the very heart of Deity.

Lest, however, we should imagine Jesus to
be a mere utterance, simply a word spoken, and
then forgotten, John is specially careful that we
should know that Jesus is a real and true Person,
and therefore he tells us that the Divine Word, of
whose fulness we have received, is most assuredly
God.

No language can be more distinct and explic-
it than that which John uses concerning Jesus. He
ascribes to Him the *eternity* which belongs alone
to God: "In the beginning was the Word." He pe-
remptorily claims *Divinity* for Him: "The Word
was God." He ascribes to Him *creative power:* "All
things were made by Him; and without Him was
not any thing made that was made." He ascribes to

Him *self-existence*, which is the essential character-
istic of God: "In Him was life." He claims for Him
a nature peculiar to God: "God is light, and in Him
is no darkness at all;" and he says that the Word
is "the true Light, which lighteth every man that
cometh into the world." No writer could be more
definite in the expressions he uses; and beyond all
question he sets forth the true and proper Deity of
that Blessed One whom we all must receive if we
would obtain eternal salvation.

Yet John does not fail to set forth that our Lord
was also man. He saith, "the Word was made
flesh," — not merely assumed manhood, but was
made flesh; made not merely man, as to His no-
bler part, His soul, but man as to His flesh, His
lower element. Our Lord was not a phantom, but
one who, as John declares in his first Epistle, could
be seen, and heard, and touched, and handled.

"The Word was made flesh, and dwelt among
us." He tabernacled with the sons of men, — a carpenter's shed His lowly refuge, and the caves and
mountains of the earth His midnight resort in His
after life. He dwelt among sinners and sufferers,
among mourners and mortals, Himself completing His citizenship among us by becoming obedient unto death, "even the death of the cross." Thus,
while He is so august a person that Heaven and
earth tremble at the majesty of His presence, yet is
He so humble a person that He is not ashamed to
call us "brethren."

XIX. THE GOD-MAN, A MIRACLE OF POWER AND LOVE

HAVE you ever thought of the miracle of power displayed in the Lord's fashioning a human body capable of union with Godhead? Our Lord Jesus Christ was incarnate in a body, which was truly a human body, but yet which was, in some wondrous way, specially prepared to sustain the indwelling of Deity. Contact with God is terrible: "He looketh on the earth, and it trembleth: He toucheth the hills, and they smoke." He puts His feet on Paran, and it melts; and Sinai dissolves in flames of fire at His presence. So strongly was this truth inwrought into the minds of the early saints, that they said, "No man can see God's face, and live;" and yet here was a manhood which did not merely see the face of God, but which was inhabited by Deity. What a wonderful human frame was this which could abide the presence of Jehovah!

Paul represents our Saviour, when He cometh into the world, as saying to His Father, "A body hast Thou prepared Me." That was indeed a body which was miraculously wrought; "that holy thing" was the special product of the Holy Spirit's supernatural power. It was a body like our own, with nerves as sensitive, and muscles as readily strained, with every organization as delicately fashioned as our own; yet God was in it. It was a frail barque to carry such a wondrous freight.

O man Christ Jesus, how couldst Thou bear the Deity within Thee? We know not how it was, but God knoweth. Let us adore this hiding of the

Almighty in human weakness, this comprehending of the Incomprehensible, this revealing of the Invisible, this localization of the Omnipresent. Human language cannot adequately set forth this unutterable truth. Suffice it to say, that the Divine power was wonderfully seen in the continued existence of the materialism of Christ's body, which else had been consumed by such a wondrous contact with Divinity as was manifested in Emmanuel, "God with us."

Christ took upon Him our nature in the fullest sense possible. His body contained everything that makes up a human body,—flesh, blood, bone, mind, heart, soul, memory, imagination, judgment,—everything that naturally belongs to a rational man. Jesus of Nazareth was the Man of men, the model representative Man. Think not of Him as a deified man any more than you would dare to regard Him as a humanized God, or demigod. Do not confound the natures that were united in Him, nor divide the Person in whom they were so marvellously blended. He is but one Person, yet as truly man as He is "very God of very God."

As you think of this truth, say, "He who sits on the throne is such as I am, sin alone excepted."

> "Oh, joy! there sitteth in our flesh,
>   Upon a throne of light,
>   One of a human mother born,
>   In perfect Godhead bright!"

Behold, what manner of love God hath bestowed upon us, that He should espouse our nature! For never had He so united Himself with any creature before. His tender mercy had ever been over all His works, but they were so distinct from Himself that an immeasurable distance separated the Creator from His creatures so far as existence and relationship are concerned. The Lord had made many noble intelligences, principalities and powers of whom we know but little; we do not

even know what those four living creatures may
be who are nearest the eternal presence; but He
had never allied Himself with any of them by actual union with His person. But, lo, He has joined
Himself to man, that creature who is made to suffer death by reason of his sin; God has come into
union with man, and therefore we may feel sure
that He loves him with amazing love, and that He
has great thoughts of good towards him. If a king's
son doth marry a member of a rebel race, then we
may be certain that there are prospects of reconciliation, pardon, and restoration for that race. There
must be, in the great heart of the Divine One, wondrous thoughts of pity and condescending love for
guilty sinners, or He would never have deigned to
take human nature into union with Himself. Let
us sound the loud cymbals of delight and thanksgiving, for the Incarnation bodes good to our race.

As God has taken manhood into union with
Himself, then God will feel for man, He will have
pity upon him, He will remember that he is dust,
He will have compassion upon his infirmities and
sicknesses. You know how truly and graciously it
is so, for that same Jesus, who was born of a woman at Bethlehem, is touched with the feeling of
our infirmities, having been in all points tempted
like as we are. Such intimate practical sympathy
would not have belonged to our great High Priest
if He had not become man. Not even though He
is Divine could He have been perfectly in sympathy with us if He had not also become bone of our
bone, and flesh of our flesh. The Captain of our
salvation could only be made "perfect through
sufferings;" and to this end, it was needful that He
should become a partaker of flesh and blood; and,
now, the Son of God can fully sympathize with
men because He is one with them in everything
except sin.

XX. ALL FULNESS IN THE GOD-MAN

In Christ Jesus, there is all fulness, "for it pleased the Father that in Him should all fulness dwell." In Him, there is everything that is essential to Deity, for "in Him dwelleth all the fulness of the Godhead." There is also, in Him, the fulness of perfect manhood, for that Godhead was revealed in Him "bodily." Partaker of flesh and blood, made in all things like unto His brethren, there was nothing lacking that was necessary to the perfection of humankind in Him. There is a fulness of atoning efficacy in His blood, for "the blood of Jesus Christ... cleanseth us from all sin." There is a fulness of justifying righteousness in His life, for "there is therefore now no condemnation to them which are in Christ Jesus." There is a fulness of Divine prevalence in His plea, for "He is able also to save them to the uttermost that come unto God by Him, seeing He ever liveth to make intercession for them."

There is a fulness of victory in His death, for "as the children are partakers of flesh and blood, He also Himself likewise took part of the same; that through death He might destroy him that had the power of death, that is, the devil." There is a fulness of efficacy in His resurrection from the dead, for by it we are "begotten again unto a lively hope, to an inheritance incorruptible, and undefiled, and that fadeth not away." There is a fulness of triumph in His ascension, for "when He ascended up on high, He led captivity captive, and gave gifts unto men."

There is, in Christ Jesus, a fulness of blessings unspeakable, unknown; a fulness of grace to pardon, of grace to regenerate, of grace to sanctify, of grace to preserve, and of grace to perfect. There is in Him a fulness at all times; a fulness by day and a fulness by night; a fulness of comfort in affliction, a fulness of guidance in prosperity, a fulness of every Divine attribute, of wisdom, of power, of love; a fulness which it is impossible to survey or to explore. There is in Him everything summed up in a grand total, as Paul says, in writing to the Ephesians, "that in the dispensation of the fulness of times He might gather together in One all things in Christ, both which are in Heaven, and which are on earth, even in Him."

"It pleased the Father that in Him should all fulness dwell." In vain we strive to recount the holy wonder; this is a theme which would exhaust an angel's powers,—the fulness which resides in Jesus our Head, and ever abides to answer our need. We may realize a little what a fulness this must be, when we think of the multitude, which no man can number, all of whom have received of His fulness, grace upon grace. There is not one of them who has received only a little grace; they are all, as Rutherford has it, "drowned debtors to His mercy;" or, as we might put it, "over head and ears" in debt to Him. They are so indebted that they will never fully know how much they owe to their Lord, but they feel that an eternal song will not be too long for the expression of their grateful praise.

Christ's fulness is an abiding fulness. John says, "Of His fulness have all we received;" yet he calls it a "fulness" still, for it never becomes any less, however many may partake of it. It was a fulness before a single sinner came to it to receive pardon; it was a fulness before a solitary saint had learned to drink of that river, the streams whereof make glad the Church of the living God; and now, after myriads, and even millions, of blood-redeemed souls have partaken of this life-giving stream, it is just as overflowing as ever. We are accustomed to say that, if a child takes a cupful of water from the sea, it is just as full as it was before; but that is not literally true, there must be just so much the less of water in the ocean. But it is literally true of Christ that, when we have not only taken out cups full,—for our needs are too great to be satisfied with such small quantities,—when we have taken out oceans full of grace,—and we need as much as that to carry us to Heaven,—there is actually as much grace left in Him as there was before we came to Him. Although we have drawn upon the exchequer of His love to an extent so boundless that we cannot comprehend it, yet there is as much mercy and grace left in Christ as there was before we began to draw from it. It is a "fulness" still, after all the saints have received of it.

There is also an abiding fulness of truth in Christ; after you have heard it for fifty years, you see more of its fulness than you did at first. Other themes weary the ear, sooner or later. I will defy any man to hold together a large congregation, year after year, with any other subject but Christ Jesus. He might attract hearers for a time; he might charm them with the discoveries of science, or with the beauties of poetry, and his oratory might be of so high an order that he might, for a while, draw the multitudes who have itching ears; but they would, in time, turn away, and say, "This is no longer to be endured; we know all he has to tell us." All music but that of Heaven becomes wearisome before long; but, oh! if the minstrel doth play upon this celestial harp, though he keepeth his fingers always among its golden strings, and be but poor and unskilled to handle an instrument so divine, yet the melody of Jesus' Name, and the sweet harmony of all His acts and attributes, will hold his listeners by the ears, and thrill their hearts as nought beside can do. The theme of Jesus' love is inexhaustible; though preachers have dwelt upon

it century after century, its freshness and fulness
still remain.

XXI. Christ Incarnate, His Knowledge of Sin

HE who came to save men is no other than God;
therefore, He is capable of viewing sin from God's
standpoint, and of understanding what was due
to God because of man's sin. By bracing His Godhead to His manhood, He was capable, in His two-
fold nature, of sustaining pangs which humanity
could not have endured apart from Godhead, and
of receiving into His infinite mind a sight of sin,
and a horror concerning it, such as no finite mind
ever could have endured.

You think, perhaps, that you comprehend sin;
but you cannot do anything of the kind. It is an evil
too monstrous for the human mind fully to know
its heights and depths, its lengths and breadths;
but Christ, who is God incarnate, fully knew what
sin meant. He had plumbed it to the very bottom,
and knew how deep it was. He had gazed upon
it, and felt all the horror of its unrighteousness,
ingratitude, and turpitude. Its sinfulness struck
His sinless mind with all its awful force, and over-
whelmed His holy soul with a horror which none
but He could bear. He was, in all respects, perfect;
and, therefore, had no need to die on His own account. It behoved Him to suffer, not because He
was the Son of God, or the Son of man; but because
He was the Redeemer, the Sponsor, the Surety, the
Substitute of men.

When I have felt the burden of my sin, I confess
that I have at times felt as if it were too great to be
taken away by any conceivable power; but, on the

other hand, when I have seen the excellence of my Master's person, the perfection of His manhood, the glory of His Godhead, the wondrous intensity of His anguish, the solid value of His obedience, I have felt as if my sin were too little a thing to need so vast a sacrifice. I have felt like John Hyatt who, when dying, said that he could not only trust Christ with his one soul, but that he could trust Him with a million souls if he had them. Were my sins greater than they are, and God forbid they should be!—were my sense of them ten thousand times more vivid than it is,—and I could wish I had a more clear and humbling consciousness of my own iniquity; yet, even then, I know that my Lord and Master is a greater Saviour than I am a sinner.

From the constitution of His person as God and man, I am certain that, if I had heaped up my iniquities till they reached the skies, though, like the giants in the ancient mythology, I had piled Pelion upon Ossa, mountain of sin upon mountain of rebellion, and had thought to scale the very throne of God in my impious rebellion, yet, even then, the precious blood of Jesus Christ, His Son, could cleanse me from all sin.

Writing to the Hebrews, concerning Christ's Incarnation, the apostle Paul says, "Once in the end of the world hath He appeared to put away sin by the sacrifice of Himself." It was He, against whom the sin had been committed, it was He, who will be the Judge of the quick and the dead, who "appeared to put away sin by the sacrifice of Himself." Is there not great comfort in this fact? It is the Son of God who has undertaken this more than Herculean labour. He appeared, sinner, to save you; God appeared, "to put away sin." Lost one, to find you, the great Shepherd has appeared; your case is not hopeless, for He has appeared. Had anybody else than God undertaken the task of putting away sin, it could never have been accomplished; but it can be accomplished now, for HE who appeared is the One with whom nothing is impossible.

Christ did not come as an amateur Saviour, trying an experiment on His own account; He came as the chosen Mediator, ordained of God for this tremendous task. He is no unauthorized individual who, of his own accord alone, stepped into the gap without orders from Heaven. No; but He appeared whom the Father had, from eternity, chosen for the great task, and whom He had commissioned and sent to perform it. His very Name, Christ, tells of His anointing for this service.

He could not sit in Heaven, and accomplish this great work of our salvation. With all reverence to the blessed Son of God, we can truly say that He could not have saved us if He had kept His throne, and not left the courts of glory; so He "appeared" on earth in human form. He "made Himself of no reputation, and took upon Him the form of a servant, and was made in the likeness of men: and being found in fashion as a man, He humbled Himself, and became obedient unto death, even the death of the cross."

XXII. Christ Incarnate, The Sinner's Only Hope

There was no hope for any sinner unless the Son of God Himself should save him. But the apostle Paul, writing to his son Timothy, says, "This is a faithful saying, and worthy of all acceptation, that Christ Jesus came into the world to save sinners." You may measure the depth of our danger by the glory of the person of Him who undertook to deliver us from it. It is the Son of God, whom angels worship, who has come "to save sinners." It must be a deep destruction from which only God Himself could rescue man.

When Christ "came into the world," observe how He had to be equipped for His service, and from His equipment learn the sternness of His task. He must be *Jesus, —a Saviour;* and then He must also be *Christ,*—anointed for the work; He must come with authority Divine, and the Spirit of God must rest upon Him to qualify Him for the great undertaking. For Paul saith not simply that *Jesus* came into the world, but *Christ Jesus*, the anointed Saviour, came that He might save. If this Divine equipment was needed, then surely the state of man was a grievous one.

Note also that Christ Jesus *came into the world* to save sinners. The Fall of man was so terrible that, if he was to be delivered from its effects, Christ Jesus must come right down into the place of our ruin; He must come to the dunghill that He might lift us out of it. God in Heaven said, "Let there be light," and the darkness fled before Him; but Christ Je-

sus must needs come into the world to save sinners; down into this polluted creation the eternal
Creator must Himself descend. He cannot save us
sinners, so great is our ruin, unless He becomes
incarnate, and takes upon Himself our nature.

And being here, think how dreadful must be
our ruin when we see that Christ cannot return
to Heaven, saying, "It is finished," until first of
all He dies. That sacred head must be crowned
with thorns, those eyes must be closed in the darkness of death, that body must be pierced even to
its heart, and then must lie in the grave, a chill,
cold corpse, ere man can be redeemed; and all that
shame, and suffering, and death were but the out-
er shell of what the Saviour suffered, for He endured the fierceness of His Father's wrath against
sin, and bare such a load as would have crushed
the whole race of men eternally had they been left
to bear it.

O sinner, you are awfully lost, you are infinitely lost, since it needs an infinite Saviour to
present the atonement of His own body in order
to save sinners from the penalty, and power, and
consequences of their sin! This is the truth which
is conveyed to us by this faithful saying, which is
"worthy of all acceptation." May the Holy Ghost
write it on our hearts!

There is one thing which should be sure to
hold, as though spellbound, the attention of every trembling sinner; it is this, — the Christ of God,
who in the end of the world has appeared, did not
come to deny the fact of human sin, or to prop-
agate a philosophy which might make sin seem
harmless, or to define it as a mere mistake, or perhaps as a calamity, but by no means as a hell-de-
serving crime. I am sure that every sensitive conscience would loathe such teaching; it could yield
no comfort whatever to a soul which had felt sin to
be exceeding sinful.

Jesus Christ did not come into the world to

help you to forget your sin. He has not come to
furnish you with a cloak with which to cover it. He
has not appeared that He may so strengthen your
minds (as some men would have you believe,) that
you may learn to laugh at your iniquities, and defy
the consequences thereof. For no such reason has
the Son of God descended from Heaven to earth.
He has come, not to lull you into a false peace, not
to whisper consolation which would turn out to be
delusive in the end, but to give you a real deliverance from sin by putting it away, and so to bring
you a true peace in which you may safely rejoice.

For, if sin be put away, then peace is lawful;
then rest of spirit becomes not only a blessing
which we may enjoy, but which we must enjoy,
and which, the more we shall enjoy it, the better
shall we please our God. O sinner, the good tidings that we bring to you, in the Gospel, are not
the mere glitter of a hope that will delude you at
the last, not a present palliative for the woe you
feel, but a real cure for all your ills, a sure and
certain deliverance from all the danger that now
hangs over you!

XXIII. Christ Incarnate, The Pledge of Deliverance

When God takes manhood into union with Himself in this matchless way, it must mean blessing to man. God cannot intend to destroy that race which He thus weds unto Himself. Such a marriage as this, between mankind and God, must foretell peace; war and destruction are never thus predicted. God incarnate in Bethlehem, to be adored by shepherds, augurs nothing but—

> "Peace on earth, and mercy mild;
> God and sinners reconciled."

O ye sinners, who tremble at the thought of the Divine wrath, as well you may, lift up your heads with joyful hope of pardon and favour, for God must be full of grace and mercy to that race which He so distinguishes above all others by taking it into union with Himself! Be of good cheer, O men of women born, and expect untold blessings, for "unto us a Child is born, unto us a Son is given."

If you look at rivers, you can often tell, by their colour, whence they have come, and the soil over which they have flowed; those which flow from melting glaciers can be recognized at once. There is a text, concerning a heavenly river, which you will understand if you look at it in this light. John, in the Revelation, says concerning the angel, "He shewed me a pure river of water of life, clear as crystal, proceeding out of the throne of God and *of the Lamb*." Where the throne is jointly occupied by God and the appointed Mediator, the incarnate

God, the once-bleeding Lamb, then the river that flows from it must be a river, not of the molten lava of devouring wrath, but of the water of life.

The consequences of Christ's Incarnation must be pleasant, profitable, saving, and ennobling to the sons of men. They include, among many other blessings, *a pledge of our deliverance*. We are a fallen race, we are sunken in the mire, we are sold under sin, in bondage and in slavery to Satan; but if God comes to our race, and espouses our nature, why, then, it must be because He has resolved to retrieve our fall. It cannot be possible for the gates of hell to enclose those who have God with them. Slaves under sin, and bondsmen beneath the law, hearken to the trump of jubilee, for One has come among you, born of a woman, made under the law, who is also "the mighty God," pledged to set you free.

He is a Saviour, and a great one; He is able to save, for He is almighty; and He is pledged to do it, for He has entered the lists on our behalf, and put on the harness for the battle. The Champion of His people is One who will not fail, nor be discouraged; the victory over all their foes shall be fully won. Jesus coming down from Heaven is the pledge that He will take His people up to Heaven; His taking our nature is the seal of our being lifted up to stand before His throne.

Were it an angel who had interposed on our behalf, we might have some fears as to the result of the conflict. Were it a mere man who had espoused our cause, we might go beyond fear, and sit down in despair; but as God has actually taken manhood into union with Himself, let us "ring the bells of Heaven," and be full of glad thanksgiving. There must be brighter and happier days in store for us, there must be salvation for man, there must be glory to God, now that we have "God with us." Let us bask in the beams of the Sun of righteousness, who now has risen upon us, a Light to lighten the

Gentiles, and to be the glory of His people Israel.

XXIV. The Incarnation, The Heart of The Gospel

God had made many visits to men before Christ's Incarnation, but the most wonderful visit of all was when He came to tarry here, some three and thirty years, to work out our salvation. What but "tender mercy", hearty mercy, intense mercy, could bring the great God to visit us so closely that He actually assumed our nature? Kings may, for various reasons, visit their subjects; but they do not think of taking upon themselves their poverty, their sickness, or their sorrow. They could not if they would, and they would not if they could; but our Divine Lord, when He came hither, took upon Him our flesh.

O children, the Lord so visited you as to become a Babe, and then a Child, who dwelt with His parents, and was subject unto them, and grew in stature, as you must do! O working-men, the Lord so visited you as to become the carpenter's Son, and to know all about your toil, and your weariness, ay, even to hunger and faintness! O sons of men, Jesus Christ has so visited you that He has assumed your nature, and taken your sicknesses, and borne your infirmities, and your iniquities, too! This was a kind of visit such as none could have thought of making save our infinitely tender and merciful Saviour. Christ Jesus, the God-Man, is our next of kin, a Brother born for adversity. In all our affliction He is afflicted; He is tenderness itself toward us.

He did not come to earth just to pay us a passing visit, but He dwelt among us in this world of sin and sorrow. This great Prince entered our abode—what if I call it this hut and hovel?— wherein our poor humanity finds its home for a season. This little planet of ours was made to burn with a superior light among its sister stars while the Creator sojourned here in human form. He trod the acres of Samaria, and traversed the hills and vales of Judæa. "He went about doing good."

He mingled among men with scarcely any reservation. Although, through His purity, He was separate from sinners as to His character, yet He was the visitor of all men. He was found eating bread with a Pharisee, which perhaps is a more wonderful thing than when He received sinners, and ate with them. A fallen woman was not too far gone in sin for Him to sit on the kerb of the well, and talk to her; nor were any of the poor and ignorant too mean for Him to care for them. His visit to us was of the most intimate kind. He disdained no man's lowliness; He turned aside from no man, however sinful he might be.

But remember that He visited us, not merely to look upon us, and to talk with us, and to teach us, and set us a high and Divine example; but He so visited us that He took upon Himself our condemnation, that He might deliver us from it. He was made a curse for us, as it is written, "Cursed is every one that hangeth on a tree." He took our debts upon Him that He might pay them, minting His own heart to create the coinage. He gave Himself for us, which is more than if I said, "He gave His blood and His life for us;" His own self He gave for us.

So graciously did He visit us that He took away with Him our ill, and left only good behind. He did not come into our nature, and yet keep Himself reserved from all the consequences of our sin; nor come into our world, and yet maintain a status superior to that of the usual denizens of it; but He

came to be a man among men, and to bear all that
train of woes which had fallen upon human nature through its departure from the ways of God.

Our Lord so visited us as to become our Surety, our Substitute, our Ransom. He hath borne
our griefs, and carried our sorrows, and the Lord
hath laid upon Him the iniquity of us all. This was
wonderful tender mercy on His part; it excels all
human conception and language. If, for the first
time, you had heard of the visit of the incarnate
God to this world, you would be struck with a
wonder which would last throughout all eternity, that God Himself should really condescend to
such a deed as this. This is the heart of the Gospel,
the incomparable fact of the Incarnation of the Son
of God, His dwelling upon the earth, and His pre-
sentation of Himself as a sacrifice unto God. Since
God has visited us, not in the form of a judge exe-
cuting vengeance, nor as an angel with a flaming
sword, but in the gentle person of that lowliest
of the lowly, who said, "Suffer the little children
to come unto Me," we are herein made to see the
tender mercy of our God. Nothing could be more
gracious than the Divine appearance upon earth
of the Man of sorrows.

XXV. The Incarnation, and Our Sonship

The Lord Jesus Christ has come in human flesh that His people might "receive the adoption of sons." What does this expression mean? Why, to feel, "Now I am under the mastery of love, as a dear child, who is both loved and loving. I go in and out of my Father's house, not as a casual servant, called in to work, and paid by the day or the week, but as a child at home. I am not looking for hire as a servant, for I am ever with my Father, and all that He has is mine. My God is my Father, and the light of His countenance makes me glad. I am not afraid of Him, but I delight in Him; and nothing can separate me from Him. I feel towards Him that perfect love which casteth out fear, and I rejoice to be owned as His child."

Try and enter into that blessed experience if you are indeed a believer in the Lord Jesus Christ, for this is why He has come in the flesh,—on purpose that you, His people, may be to the full the adopted children of the Lord, receiving and enjoying all the privileges which sonship secures to you.

Then, next, exercise your heirship. One who is a son, and who knows that he is the heir of all his father's estates, does not pine in poverty, nor act like a beggar. He looks upon everything that his father possesses as being his own; he regards his father's wealth as making him rich. He does not feel that he is stealing if he takes what his father has made to be his own, but he makes free with it.

I wish believers would make free with the

promises and blessings of their God. Help yourselves to all that He has laid up in store for you, for
no good thing will the Lord withhold from you if
you walk uprightly. All things are yours: you only
need to use the hand of faith, and so to take possession of them. If you appropriate a promise of
your Father's, it will not be pilfering; you may take
it boldly, and say, "This is mine." Your adoption
into the family of God brings with it large rights;
be not slow to claim them. Paul writes to the Ro-
mans, "The Spirit itself beareth witness with our
spirit, that we are the children of God: and if children, then heirs; heirs of God, and joint-heirs with
Christ."

Among men, sons are only heirs in anticipation so long as their fathers are alive; they only
become heirs in possession when their fathers are
dead. But our Father in Heaven lives, yet we have
the full privileges of heirship in Him even now.
The Lord Jesus Christ was made of a woman on
purpose that His dear people might at once enter
into their heirship.

You ought to feel a sweet joy in the perpetual relationship which is now established between
you and God, for Jesus is still your Brother. You
have been adopted by God, and He has never can-
celled that adoption yet. There is such a thing as
regeneration, but there is not such a thing as the
life then received dying out. If you are born unto
God, you are born unto God. The stars may turn to
coals, and the sun and moon may become clots of
blood, but he that is born of God has a life within
him which can never end; he is God's child, and
God's child he shall be for ever. Therefore let him
walk at large like a child, an heir, a prince of the
blood royal of Heaven, who bears a relationship to
the Lord which neither time nor eternity can ever
destroy.

XXVI. The Incarnation, Its Glory

There was great glory about our Lord Jesus Christ even in His state of humiliation. Go back in thought to that memorable period, and try to realize what then happened.

See, Jesus is born of lowly parents, laid in a manger, and wrapped in swaddling-bands; but, lo! the principalities and powers in the heavenly places are all in commotion concerning this unparalleled event. First, one angel descends to proclaim the advent of the newborn King, and suddenly there is with him a multitude of the heavenly host singing, "Glory to God in the highest, and on earth peace, good will toward men."

Nor is the commotion confined to the spirits above; for in the heavens which overhang this earth there is a stir. A bright particular star is deputed to appear on behalf of all the stars, as if it were the envoy and plenipotentiary of all worlds to represent them before their King. This star is put in commission to wait upon the Lord, to be His herald to men afar off, His usher to conduct them to His presence, and His body-guard to sentinel His cradle.

I suppose you have each one his own imagination as to what this star was. It would seem to have been altogether supernatural, and not a star, or a comet of the ordinary kind. It was not a constellation, nor a singular conjunction of planets; there is nothing in the Scriptures to support such a conjecture. In all probability, it was not a star in the sense

in which we now speak of stars; for we find that
it moved before the wise men, then suddenly dis-
appeared, and again shone forth to move before
them. It could not have been a star in the upper
spheres like others, for such movements would
not have been possible. If the star was in its zenith
over Bethlehem, it would have been in its zenith
over Jerusalem, too; for the distance between them
is so small that it would not have been possible to
observe any difference in the position of the star in
the two places. It must have been a star occupying
quite another sphere from that in which the planets revolve.

We believe it to have been a luminous appearance in mid-air; probably akin to that which led the
children of Israel through the wilderness, which
was a pillar of cloud by day and a pillar of fire by
night. Whether it was seen in the daylight or not,
we cannot tell. Chrysostom and the early fathers
are wonderfully positive about many things which
Scripture leaves in doubt; but as these eminent di-
vines drew upon their imagination for their facts,
we are not under bonds to follow them. They aver
that this star was so bright as to be visible all day
long. If so, we can imagine the wise men travelling
day and night; but if it could be seen only by night,
the picture before us grows far more singular and
weird-like as we see these Easterns quietly pursu-
ing their star-lit way, resting *perforce* when the sun
was up, but noiselessly hurrying at night through
slumbering lands.

But, whatever it may have been, it was the
means of guiding to the Saviour, from far-off
lands, the most studious minds of the age. Making
a long and difficult journey, these representatives
of the Gentiles at last arrive at the place where the
young Child is. Lo! the kings of Seba and Sheba
offer gifts, — "gold, and frankincense, and myrrh."
Wise men, the leaders of their peoples, bow down
before Him, and pay homage to the Son of God.

Wherever Christ is, He is honourable. "Unto you that believe He is an honour." Even in the day of small things, when He is denied such entertainment as He deserves, and is hidden away with things which are despised, He is still most glorious. Christ, though a Child, is still King of kings; though among the oxen, He is still distinguished by His star.

It would not be possible to tell how far off the native country of these wise men lay; it may have been so distant that the journey occupied nearly the whole of the two years of which they spake concerning the appearance of the star. Travelling was slow in those days, surrounded with difficulties and dangers. They may have come from Persia, or India, or Tartary, or even from the mysterious land of Sinim, now known to us as China. If so, strange and uncouth must have been the speech of those who worshipped around the young Child at Bethlehem, yet needed He no interpreter to understand and accept their adoration.

Why was the birth of the King of the Jews made known to these foreigners, and not to those nearer home? Why did the Lord select those who were so many hundreds of miles away, while the children of the kingdom, in whose very midst the Saviour was brought forth, were yet strangely ignorant of His presence? See here again another instance of the sovereignty of God. Both in shepherds and in Eastern magi gathering around the young Child, I see God dispensing His favours as He wills; and, as I see it, I exclaim, "Even so, Father; for so it seemed good in Thy sight." As of old, there were many widows in Israel in the days of Elias the prophet, yet unto none of them was he sent, but unto the woman of Sarepta, a city of Sidon, so there were many among the Jews who were called wise men, but unto none of them did the star appear; but it shone on Gentile eyes, and led a chosen company from the ends of the earth to bow at Emmanuel's feet.

Sovereignty, in these cases, clothed itself in the robes of mercy. It was great mercy that regarded the low estate of the shepherds, and it was far-reaching mercy which gathered from lands which lay in darkness a company of men made wise unto salvation. Mercy, wearing her resplendent jewels, was present with Divine sovereignty in the lowly abode of Bethlehem. Is it not a delightful thought that, around the cradle of the Saviour, as well as around His throne in Heaven, these two attributes meet? He makes Himself known,—and herein is mercy; but it is to those whom He has chosen,—and herein He shows that He will have mercy on whom He will have mercy, and He will have compassion on whom He will have compassion.

XXVII. THE WISE MEN AND THE INCARNATION

As soon as the wise men came to Jerusalem, they enquired, "Where is He that is born King of the Jews?" They were fully convinced that He was the King of the Jews, and that He had been but recently born, so they asked, "Where is He?"

In the case of these wise men, we see *ignorance admitted*. Truly wise men are never above asking questions, because they are wise men. Persons who have taken the name and degree of wise men, and are so esteemed, sometimes think it beneath them to confess any degree of ignorance, but the really wise think not so; they are too well instructed to be ignorant of their own ignorance. Many men might have been wise if they had but been aware that they were fools. The knowledge of our ignorance is the doorstep of the temple of knowledge. Some think they know, and therefore never know. Had they known that they were blind, they would soon have been made to see; but because they say, "We see," therefore their blindness remains upon them.

The wise men were not content with admitting their ignorance; but, in their case, there was *information entreated*. They thought it likeliest that Jesus would be known at the metropolitan city. Was He not the King of the Jews? Where, then, would He be so well known as at the capital? They probably asked the guards at the gate, "Where is He that is born King of the Jews?" But the guards laughed them to scorn, and replied, "We know no king but

Herod." Perhaps they met a loiterer in the streets, and to him they said, "Where is He that is born King of the Jews?" and he answered, "What care I for such crazy questions? I am looking for a companion who will drink with me." Possibly, they asked a trader; but he sneered, and said, "Never mind kings, what will you buy, or what have you to sell?" "Where is He that is born King of the Jews?" said they to a Sadducee, and he replied, "Be not such fools as to talk in that fashion; or if you do, pray call on my religious friend, the Pharisee." They passed a woman in the streets, and asked, "Where is He that is born King of the Jews?" but she said, "My child is sick at home, I have enough to do to think of my poor babe; I care not who is born, or who beside may die." When they went to the very highest quarters, they obtained but little information; yet they were not content till they had learned all that could be known concerning the new-born King.

They were not satisfied with merely getting to Jerusalem. They might have said, "Ah! now we are in the land where the Child is born, we will be thankful, and sit down contentedly." They heard that He was born at Bethlehem, so they journeyed thither; but we do not find that, when they reached that village, they said, "This is a favoured spot, we will sit down here." Not at all; they wanted to know where the house was in which they could find the King whom they had come so far to seek. They saw the star stand still above the village inn, and they knew by that sign that the new-born King was there, but that did not satisfy them. No; they rested not till they saw the Child Himself, and worshipped Him.

XXVIII. THE WISE MEN, WHAT THEY TEACH US

THERE is much to be learned from the action of these wise men; so let us, in thought, follow them. They have come to the house where the young Child is. What will they do? Will they stand still, and look at the star? No; *they enter in*. The star still shines, but they are not afraid of losing its radiance, for they have come where they can behold the Sun of righteousness. They lift the latch, and enter the lowly residence of the Babe. They see the star no longer, and they have no need to see it, for there is "He that is born King of the Jews." Now the true Light has shone upon them from the face of the Child; they behold the incarnate God.

How wise you will be if, when you have been led to the place where Christ is, by any man, you do not rest in his leadership, but resolve to see Christ for yourselves! How much I long that you may enter into the fellowship of the mystery, pass through the door, and come and behold the young Child, and bow before Him! Our sorrow is that so many are so unwise as to be content with seeing us. We are only their guides, but they are apt to make us their end. We point the way, but they do not follow the road; they stand gazing upon us. It was not so with the wise men. The star had done its work, and passed away; but Jesus remained, and they came unto Him.

These men proved that they were wise because, when they saw the Child, *they worshipped Him*. Theirs was not curiosity gratified, but de-

votion exercised. We, too, must worship the Saviour, or we shall never be saved by Him. He has
not come to put away our sins, and yet to leave us
ungodly and self-willed. Oh, you who have never
worshipped the Christ of God, may you be led to
do so! He is God; therefore, adore Him.

Was God ever seen in such a worshipful form
before? Behold, He bows the heavens; He rides
upon the wings of the wind; He scatters flames of
fire; He speaks, and His dread artillery shakes the
hills. Who would not adore the great and terrible
Jehovah? But is it not much better to behold Him
here, allied to your nature, wrapped like other
babes in swaddling-clothes, tender, feeble, next of
kin to your own self? Will you not worship God
when He thus comes down to you, and becomes
your Brother, born for your salvation?

You cannot properly worship a Christ whom
you do not know; but when you think of Jesus
Christ, whose goings forth were of old, from everlasting, the eternally-begotten Son of the Father,
and then see Him coming here to be a man of the
substance of His mother, and know and understand why He came, and what He did when He
came, then you fall down, and worship Him.

> "Son of God, to Thee we bow,
>   Thou art Lord, and only Thou;
>   Thou the woman's promised seed;
>   Thou who didst for sinners bleed."

We worship "Jesus of Nazareth, the King of the
Jews." Our faith sees Him go from the manger to
the cross, and from the cross right up to the throne;
and there, where Jehovah dwells, amidst the in-
sufferable glory of the Divine presence, stands the
very same Person who slept in the manger at Bethlehem; there He reigns as King of kings and Lord
of lords. Our souls worship Him. Thou art our
Prophet; every word Thou sayest, we believe, and
desire to obey. Thou art our Priest; Thy sacrifice

hath made us free from guilt, we are washed white in the fountain of Thy blood. Thou art our King; give Thy commands, and we will obey them; lead Thou on, and we will follow. Thou art God, and we worship Thee.

After worshipping Christ, the wise men *presented their gifts* to Him. One broke open his casket of gold, and laid it at the feet of the new-born King. Another presented frankincense,—one of the precious products of the country from which they came; and others laid myrrh at the Redeemer's feet. All these they gave to Him to prove the sincerity of their worship; they gave substantial offerings with no niggard hand.

These wise men, when they worshipped Christ, did not permit it to be a mere empty-handed adoration; and truly wise men are still liberal men. Consecration is the best education. It is thought, by some, to be wise to be always receiving; but our Saviour said, "It is more blessed to give than to receive."

God judges our hearts by that which spontaneously comes from them; hence, the "sweet cane bought with money" is acceptable to Him when given freely. He doth not tax His saints for His offerings, nor weary them with His demands for incense; but He delights to see in them that true love which cannot express itself in mere words, but must use gold, and frankincense, and myrrh,—works of love and deeds of self-denial and generosity,—to be the emblems of its gratitude. We shall never get into the heart of happiness till we become unselfish and generous; we have but chewed the husks of religion, which are often bitter; we have never eaten of the sweet kernel until we have felt the love of God constraining us to make sacrifices for Him. There is nothing in the true believer's power which he would not do for his Lord; nothing in our substance which we would not give to Him, nothing in ourselves which we would not devote to His service.

XXIX. The Incarnation, the Cause of Trouble

When Christ was born, *many were troubled because of Him*. Matthew says that "Herod was troubled, and all Jerusalem with him." It is an unusual thing to hear of a king being troubled by a babe. Proud Herod, the fire-eater, troubled by a babe in swaddling-bands, lying in a manger? Ah, me! how little is the real greatness of wickedness, and how small a power of goodness may bring it grief!

When some people hear the Gospel, and find that it has power in it, they are troubled. Herod was troubled, because he feared that he should lose his throne; he thought that the house of David, in the person of the new-born Child, would take possession of his throne; so he trembled, and was troubled. How many there are still who think that, if religion be true, they will lose by it! Business will suffer. There are some businesses that ought to suffer; and as true godliness spreads, they will suffer. I need not indicate them; but those who are engaged in them usually feel that they had better cry out, "Great is Diana of the Ephesians," for they get their living by making and selling her shrines; and if their shrines are in danger, and their craft is in danger, then they are troubled. I have known men, who have been ringleaders in sin, and they have thought that they should lose some of their followers through Christ's coming; so they have been troubled.

But "all Jerusalem" was troubled with Herod. Why was that? It was most probably because the people thought there would be contention. If there was a new King born, there would be a fight between Him and Herod, and there would be trouble for Jerusalem. So there are some men who say, "Do not bring that religion here; it makes such contention. One believes this, and one believes that, and another believes nothing at all. We shall have trouble in the family if we get religion into it." Yes, you will; that is acknowledged in the Scriptures, for our Lord came to bring fire on the earth. He has come, with a sword in His hand, on purpose to fight against everything that is evil; and there must, therefore, be contention. Hence I do not wonder that the lovers of ease are troubled.

Yet it is very sad that the Gospel, which is meant to be good news to men, should trouble them; that the heavenly offer of free grace should trouble them; that to have Heaven's gate widely opened before them should trouble them; that to be asked to wash themselves or to be washed in the blood of Christ should trouble them. Troubled by infinite mercy! Troubled by almighty love! Yet such is the depravity of human nature that, to many who hear the Gospel every day, it is still nothing but a trouble to them.

Herod tried to get out of the trouble by playing the part of a hypocrite. "Yes," he says to the wise men, "there is One who is born King of the Jews. Will you kindly tell me all about it? You say that you saw a star; when did it appear? Be very precise in your account of it. Did you take note of its movements? What time in the evening was it first visible? What day of the month did it appear?"

Herod is very particular in getting all the information that he can about the star; and now he sends for the doctors of divinity, and the scribes, and the priests, and he says to them, "When ought this Messiah, that you talk about, to be born, and where ought He to be born? Tell me." Herod, you see, is a wonderful disciple, is he not? He is sitting at the feet of the doctors; he is willing to be instructed by the magi; and then he finishes up by saying to the wise men, "You go and worship the new-born King; you are quite right to have come all this distance to worship this Child. Be particular, too, to take notes as to where you find Him, and then come and tell me about Him, that I also may go and worship Him."

So we always find that, where Christ is, there is a Herod or a Judas somewhere near. If the Gospel comes to any place, there is a certain number of persons who say, "Oh, yes, yes, yes, we shall attend that place!" I know a certain town where there is one true preacher of the Gospel, who has won many to Christ; but there are a great many who go there who know nothing at all about Christ. A certain number of people would think that all was wrong with them if they did not hear sound doctrine; but all the while they have made up their minds that sound doctrine shall never change their lives, and shall never affect their inward character. They are hypocrites, just as this man Herod was. They will not have Christ to reign over them. They do not mind hearing about Him; they do not mind acknowledging to a certain extent His rights; but they will not yield allegiance to Him, they will not practically submit to His rule, and become believers in Him, and followers of Him.

XXX. The Incarnation, Also a Source of Joy

Though the coming of Christ was the cause of trouble to the ungodly, it is, to us who are His own people, a wellspring of pure, unmingled joy. We associate with His crucifixion much of sorrowful regret, but we derive from His birth at Bethlehem nothing but delight. The angelic song was a fit accompaniment to the joyful event, and the filling of the whole earth with peace and good will is the appropriate consequence of the gracious condescension which made it an accomplished fact. The stars of Bethlehem cast no baleful light. We may sing, with undivided joy, "Unto us a Child is born, unto us a Son is given."

When the Eternal stooped from Heaven, and assumed the nature of His own creature who had rebelled against Him, the deed could mean no harm to man. God in our nature is not God against us, but God with us. We may take up the young Child in our arms, and feel, with old Simeon, that we have seen the Lord's salvation.

Christ's Incarnation cannot mean destruction to men. I do not wonder that the men of the world celebrate the supposed anniversary of the great birthday as a high festival with carols and banquets. Knowing nothing of the spiritual meaning of the mystery, they yet perceive that it means man's good, and so, in their own rough way, they respond to it. We, who observe no days which are not appointed of the Lord, rejoice continually in the advent of the Prince of peace, and find in our

Lord's manhood a fountain of consolation.

To those of us who are truly the people of God, the Incarnation is the subject of a thoughtful joy, which ever increases with our knowledge of its meaning, even as rivers are enlarged by many trickling brooks. The birth of Jesus not only brings us hope, but the certainty of good things. We do not merely speak of Christ's coming into relation with our nature, but of His entering into union with ourselves, for He has become one flesh with us for purposes as great as His love. He is one with all of us who have believed in His Name.

If you have believed in Him, you ought to feel a joyful satisfaction in the assurance that Christ became Incarnate in order that He might enable us to enjoy the fulness of the privilege of adoption into the family of His Father, who says to all believers, "I will receive you, and will be a Father unto you, and ye shall be My sons and daughters, saith the Lord Almighty." Well may we rejoice if He has spoken thus to us.

XXXI. THE INCARNATION, ACCORDING TO PROPHECY

IN every particular, the birth of Christ was the fulfilment of ancient prophecies. Isaiah had foretold
the miraculous conception: "Behold, a virgin shall
conceive, and bear a Son." This expression is unparalleled even in Sacred Writ; of no other woman
could it be said beside the Virgin Mary, and of no
other man could it be written that his mother was
a virgin. The Greek word and the Hebrew are both
very expressive of the true and real virginity of the
mother, to show us that Jesus Christ was born of
woman, and not of man. Just as the woman, by
her venturous spirit, stepped first into transgression, — lest she should be despised and trampled
on, God in His wisdom devised that the woman, and the woman alone, should be the author
of the body of the God-Man who should redeem
mankind. Albeit that she herself first tasted the
accursed fruit, and tempted her husband, (it may
be that Adam out of love to her tasted that fruit,)
lest she should be degraded, lest she should not
stand on an equality with him, God hath ordained
that His Son should be sent forth "born of a woman," and the first promise was that the seed of the
woman, not the seed of the man, should bruise the
serpent's head.

Moreover, there was a peculiar wisdom or-
daining that Jesus Christ should be the Son of the
woman, and not of the man, because, had He been
born of the flesh, "that which is born of the flesh is
flesh," and merely flesh, and He would naturally,

by carnal generation, have inherited all the frailties and the sins and the infirmities which man hath from his birth; He would have been conceived in sin, and shapen in iniquity, even as the rest of us. Therefore He was not born of man; but the Holy Ghost overshadowed the Virgin Mary, and Christ stands as the only man, save one other, who came forth pure from His Maker's hands, who could ever say, "I am pure." Ay, and He could say far more than that other Adam could say concerning his purity, for He maintained His integrity, and never let it go; and from His birth down to His death He knew no sin, neither was guile found in His mouth.

Oh, marvellous sight! Let us stand and look at it. A child of a virgin, what a mixture! There is the finite and the Infinite, there is the mortal and the Immortal, corruption and Incorruption, the manhood and the Godhead, time married to eternity, God linked with a creature, the infinity of the august Maker come to tabernacle on this speck of earth; the vast unbounded One, whom earth could not hold, and the heavens cannot contain, lying in His mother's arms; He who fastened the pillars of the universe, and riveted the nails of creation, hanging on a mortal breast, depending on a creature for nourishment. Oh, miraculous conception! Oh, marvellous birth! Verily, angels may wish to look into a subject too mysterious for us to comprehend.

Isaiah did not say, "A princess shall conceive, and bear a Son," but a virgin. Her virginity was her highest honour. True, she was of royal lineage; she could reckon David and Solomon amongst her ancestors. Nor was she, in point of intellect, an inferior woman. I take it that she had great strength of mind, otherwise she could not have composed so sweet a piece of poetry as that which is called the Virgin's Song, beginning, "My soul doth magnify the Lord." She is not a person to be despised by Protestants. Because Roman Catholics pay too much respect to the Virgin Mary, and offer prayers to her, we are apt to speak of her in a slighting manner. She ought not to be placed under the ban of contempt, for she could truly sing, "From henceforth all generations shall call me blessed." I suppose Protestant generations are amongst the "all generations" who ought to call her blessed. Her name is Mary, and quaint George Herbert wrote an anagram upon it, —

> "How well her name an ARMY doth present,
> In whom the Lord of hosts did pitch His tent."

Though she was not a princess, yet her name, Mary, by interpretation, signifies a princess; and though she is not the queen of Heaven, yet she has a right to be reckoned amongst the queens of earth; and though she is not the lady of our Lord, she does walk amongst the renowned and mighty women of Scripture.

Yet Jesus Christ's birth was a humble one. The Lord of glory was not born in a palace, but in a stable. Princes, Christ owes you nothing; He is not your debtor. He was not wrapped in purple, ye had not prepared a golden cradle for Him to be rocked in. And ye mighty cities, which then were great and famous, your marble halls were not blessed with His little footsteps! He came out of a village, poor and despised, even Bethlehem; when there, He was not born in the governor's house or in the mansion of the chief man, but in a manger. Tradition tells us that His manger was cut in the solid rock; there was He laid, and the oxen likely enough came to feed from the self-same manger, the hay and the fodder of which formed His only bed. Oh! wondrous condescension, that our blessed Jesus should be girded with humility, and stoop so low!

But let us take courage from this fact. If Jesus Christ was born in a manger in a rock, why should He not come and live in our rocky hearts? If He was born in a stable, why should not the stable of our souls be made into a habitation for Him? If He was born in poverty, may not the poor in spirit expect that He will be their Friend? If He thus endured degradation at the first, will He count it any dishonour to come to the very poorest and humblest of His creatures, and tabernacle in the souls of His children? Oh, no! we can gather a lesson of comfort from His humble parentage, and we can rejoice that not a queen, or an empress, but that a humble woman became the mother of the Lord of glory.

Our Lord was so poor that His mother, when she had to redeem Him, could not bring a lamb, which was the sacrifice for all who could afford it, but she presented the poorer offering, a pair of turtle doves or two young pigeons, and so she came as a poor woman, and He was presented to the Lord as a poor woman's Child. Herein lies rich comfort for lowly hearts. When I think of the Prince of glory and the Lord of angels stooping so low as this, that a poor woman bears Him in her arms, and calls Him her Babe, surely there must be salvation for the lowest, the poorest, and the most sunken. When the all-glorious Lord, in order to be incarnate, is born of a poor woman, and publicly acknowledged as a poor woman's Child, we feel sure that He will receive the poorest and most despised when they seek His face. Yes, Jesus, the Son of the carpenter, means salvation to carpenters and all others of lowly rank.

XXXII. CHRIST'S POVERTY, OUR RICHES

THERE was no need that Christ should be poor except for our sakes. Some persons always have been poor, and it seems as if, with all their struggles, they could never rise out of poverty; but of our Lord Jesus Christ it can truly be said that "He was rich." Shall I take you back, in thought, to the glories of the eternity when, as very God of very God, He dwelt in the bosom of the Father? He was so rich that He was not dependent upon any of the angels He had created, nor did He rely for glory upon any of the works of His hands. Truly, Heaven was His abode; but He could have made ten thousand Heavens if He had willed to do so. All the greatest wonders He had ever made were but specimens of others that He could make whenever He pleased to do so.

He had all possibility of inconceivable and immeasurable wealth within His power; yet He laid aside all that, denied Himself the power to enrich Himself, and came down to earth that He might save and bless us. His poverty was all voluntary; there was a necessity laid upon Him, but the sole necessity was His own love. There was no need, as far as He was concerned, that He should ever be poor; the only need was because we were in need, and He loved us so that He would rescue us from poverty, and make us eternally rich.

Our Lord's was also very emphatic poverty. I believe that it is quite true that no one knows the pinch of poverty like a person who has once been rich. It is your fallen emperor, who has to beg his bread, who knows what beggary is. It is the man who once possessed broad acres, who at last has to hire a lodging in a miserable garret, who knows what abject poverty is. So was it with the Saviour. He had been emphatically rich. You cannot press into the word "rich" all that Jesus was; you have to feel that it is a very poor word, even though it be rich, with which to describe His heavenly condition. He was emphatically rich; and so, when He descended into poverty, it was poverty with an emphasis laid upon it, the contrast was so great. The difference between the richest and the poorest man is just nothing compared with the difference between Christ in the glory of His Godhead and Christ in His humiliation, the stoop was altogether immeasurable. You cannot describe His riches, and you cannot describe His poverty. You have never had any idea of how high He was as God; and you can never imagine how low He stooped when He cried, "My God, My God, why hast Thou forsaken Me?"

It was great poverty to Christ to be a man. Humanity is a poor thing when you set it in comparison with the Deity. What a narrow space does man fill! But God is infinite. What a little can man do! Yet God is omnipotent. How little does man know! And God is omniscient. How confined is man to a single spot! And God is omnipresent! I say not that Jesus ever ceased to be God, but we do remember that He became man; and in becoming man, He became poor in comparison with His condition as God.

But then, as man, He was also a poor man. He might have been born in marble halls, swaying the sceptre of universal empire, and from His birth receiving the homage of all mankind. But instead of that, you know, He was reputed to be the carpenter's Son, His mother was but a humble Jewish maid, and His birthplace was a stable, —

poor accommodation for the Prince of the kings of the earth. His early life was spent in a carpenter's shop; and afterwards His companions were mostly poor fishermen, and for His maintenance He was dependent upon the alms of His followers.

The apostle Paul, writing to the church of God at Corinth, and to all who call upon the Name of Jesus Christ, said, "For your sakes He became poor, that ye through His poverty might be rich." Then, if Christ's poverty be such as I have tried to describe it, what must the riches of His people be? If our riches are proportionate to His poverty, what rich people we are! He was as poor as poor can be; and we, if we are believing in Him, are as rich as rich can be. So low as He went, so high do we rise. That is how the scales of the sanctuary act; as He sinks, we go up.

XXXIII. Christ's Body Divinely Prepared

THAT is a very remarkable expression that Paul represents our Saviour as using in Hebrews 10:5: "When He cometh into the world, He saith, Sacrifice and offering Thou wouldest not, but a body hast Thou prepared Me." The body of Christ was specially prepared for Him and for His great work. To begin with, it was a sinless body, without taint of original sin, else God could not have dwelt therein. It was a body made highly vital and sensitive, probably far beyond what ours are; for sin has a blunting and hardening effect even upon flesh; and Christ's flesh, though He was made "in the likeness of sinful flesh," was not sinful flesh, but flesh which yielded prompt obedience to His spirit. His body was capable of great endurance, so as to know the griefs and agonies and unspeakable sorrows of a delicate, holy, and tender kind which it was necessary for Him to bear. In the fulness of time, He came into that body, which was admirably adapted to enshrine the Godhead.

He who assumed that body was existent before that body was prepared. He says, "A body hast Thou prepared Me. Lo, I come." We could not, any one of us, have said that a body was prepared for us, and therefore we would come to it; for we had no existence before our bodies were fashioned. From everlasting to everlasting, our Lord Jesus is God, and He comes out of eternity into time, the Father bringing Him into the world, to fulfil the great purposes of His love and grace. He was before all

worlds, and therefore He was before He came into
this world to dwell for a while in His prepared
body.

Beloved, *the human nature of Christ was taken on
Him in order that He might be able to do for us that
which God desired and required*. God desired to see
an obedient man, a man who would keep His law
to the full; and He sees him in Christ. God desired
to see one who would vindicate the eternal justice,
and show that sin is no trifle; and behold our Lord,
the eternal Son of God, entering into that prepared
body, was ready to do all this mighty work, by
rendering to the law a full recompense for our dishonour of it. He renders unto God an absolutely
perfect righteousness; as the second Adam, the
Lord from Heaven, He presents it to His Father for
all whom He represents.

He bows His head a victim beneath Jehovah's
sword, that the truth, and justice, and honour of
God might suffer no detriment. His body was
"prepared" to this end. Incarnation is a means to
atonement. Only a man could vindicate the law,
and therefore the Son of God became a man. This is
a wonderful Being, this God in our nature. Surely,
for the Incarnation and the Atonement, the world
was made from the first. Was this the reason why
the morning stars sang together when they saw
the corner-stone of the world laid, because they
had an inkling that, here, God would be manifest
as nowhere else beside, and the Creator would be
wedded to the creature? That God might be manifested in the Christ, it may even be that sin was
permitted. Assuredly, there could have been no
sacrifice on Calvary if there had not first of all been
sin in Eden. The whole scheme, the whole of God's
decrees and acts, worked up to the consummation
of an atoning Saviour.

Of the great pyramid of Creation and Providence, Christ is the apex. He is the flower of all
that God hath made. His Divine nature, in strange

union with humanity, constitutes a peerless Personage, such as never was before, and can never be again. God in our nature one Being, yet wearing two natures, is altogether unique. He saith, "A body hast Thou prepared Me. Lo, I come."

XXXIV. Jesus Christ, His Own Herald

"Lo, I come," saith Christ; so He is His own herald. He does not wait for an eloquent preacher to act as master of the ceremonies to Him; He introduces Himself. You need not do anything to draw Christ's attention to you; it is Christ who draws attention to Himself. Do you see this? You are the blind bat; and He is all eye towards you, and bids you look on Him. He bids you look on Him when you beseech Him to look on you.

To many men and women, Christ has come though they have not even desired Him. Yea, He has come even to those who have hated Him. Saul of Tarsus was on his way to worry the saints at Damascus, but Jesus said, "Lo, I come;" and when He looked out of Heaven, He turned Saul, the persecutor, into Paul, the apostle. Again and again has that gracious word been fulfilled, "I was found of them that sought Me not; I was made manifest unto them that asked not after Me." Herein is the glorious sovereignty of His love fully exercised, and grace reigns supreme. "Lo, I come," is the announcement of majestic grace which waiteth not for man, neither tarrieth for the sons of men.

Before He came, He delighted in the thought of His Incarnation. The Supreme Wisdom saith, "My delights were with the sons of men." Happy in His Father's courts, He yet looked forward to an access of happiness in becoming man. "Can that be?" saith one. Could the Son of God be happier than He was in Heaven? As God, He was infinitely blessed; but He knew nothing by experience of the life of man, and into that sphere He desired to enter. To the Godhead, there can be no enlargement, for it is infinite; but, still, there can be an addition; our Lord was to add the nature of man to that of God. He would live as man, suffer as man, and triumph as man, and yet remain God; and to this He looked forward with a strange delight, inexplicable except upon the knowledge of the great love He bore to us. He had given His heart so entirely to His dear bride, whom He saw in the glass of predestination, that for her He would endure all things.

> "Yea, saith the Lord, for her I'll go
>   Through all the depths of care and woe,
> And on the cross will even dare
>   The bitter pangs of death to bear."

It was wondrous love. Our Lord's love surpasses all language and even thought.

When He appears, it is as the personal Lord. Lay the stress upon the pronoun, "Lo, *I* come." The infinite *Ego* appears, "Lo, *I* come." No mere man could talk thus, and be sane. No servant or prophet of God would ever say, "Lo, I come." Saintly men talk not so. God's prophets and apostles have a modest sense of their true position; they never magnify themselves, though they magnify their office. It is for God alone to say, "Lo, I come." He who says it takes the body prepared for Him, and comes in His own proper personality as the I AM. He comes forth from the ivory palaces to inhabit the tents of manhood, and He stands forth, in His matchless personality, ready to do the will of God.

"Lo, I come." This is no dirge; I think I hear a silver trumpet ring out, "Lo, I come." These words indicate a joyful alacrity and intense eagerness. The coming of the Saviour was to Him a thing of exceeding willingness. "For the joy that was set before Him, He endured the cross, despising the shame." This is no clandestine union. He bids Heaven behold Him come into our nature, and calls upon all on earth to gaze upon the wondrous mystery.

Our Lord Jesus is the way to Himself. Did you ever notice that? He Himself comes to us, and so He is the way by which we meet Him. He says, "I am the way." He is our rest, and the way to our rest. You say that you want to know how to get to Christ. You have not to get to Him, for He has come to you. It is well for you to come to Christ; but that is only possible because Christ has come to you. Jesus is near you; near you *now*. Backslider, He comes to you! Wandering soul, roving to the very brink of perdition, the good Shepherd cries, "Lo, I come."

Remember, also, that *He is the blessing which He brings*. Jesus not only gives life and resurrection, but He says, "I am the resurrection and the life." Christ is salvation, and everything needful to salvation is in Him. If He comes, all good comes *with* Him, or rather *in* Him. An enquirer once said to a minister, "The next step for me is to get a deeper conviction of sin." The minister replied, "No such thing, my friend; the next step is to trust in Jesus, for He says, Come unto Me." To come to Jesus, or rather to receive Jesus who has come to us, is the one essential step into eternal salvation.

Though our Lord does say, "Come unto Me," He has preceded it with this other word, "Lo, I come." Poor cripple, if you cannot come to Jesus, ask Him to come to you; and He will. Here you lie, and you have been for years in this case; you have no man to put you into the pool, and it would do you no good if he did; but Jesus can make you whole, and He is here. You cannot stir hand or foot because of spiritual paralysis; but your case is not hopeless. Jesus says, "Lo, I come." He has no paralysis. He can come, leaping over the mountains of division. I know that my Lord came to me, or I should never have come to Him; then, why should He not come to you? I came to Him because He came to me.

> "He drew me, and I followed on,
>   Charmed to confess the voice Divine."

Why should He not draw you also? Is He not doing so? Yield to the pressure of His love.

XXXV. Jesus Christ, "Full of Grace and Truth"

In describing the coming of Christ, John says, "The Word was made flesh, and dwelt among us, (and we beheld His glory, the glory as of the only begotten of the Father,) full of grace and truth." In Jesus Christ, all the attributes of God are seen; veiled, but yet verily there. You have only to read the Gospels, and to look with willing eyes, and you shall behold in Christ all that can possibly be seen of God. It is veiled in human flesh, as it must be; for the glory of God is not to be seen by us absolutely. It is toned down to these dim eyes of ours; but the Godhead is there, the perfect Godhead in union with the perfect manhood of Christ Jesus our Lord, to whom be glory for ever and ever.

The two Divine things which are more clearly seen in Jesus than aught else are "grace and truth." Christ did not simply come to tell us about grace, but actually to bring us grace. He is not merely full of the news of grace and truth, but of grace and truth themselves. Others had been messengers of gracious tidings, but He came to bring grace. Others teach us truth, but Jesus is the truth. He is that grace and truth whereof others spake. Jesus is not merely a Teacher, an Exhorter, a Worker of grace and truth; but these heavenly things are in Him, and He is full of them.

Christ has brought us grace in rivers and truth in streams; and the two rivers unite in the one fulness of grace and truth. That is to say, the grace is truthful grace; not grace in fiction, or in fancy, not grace to be hoped for or to be dreamed of, but grace every atom of which is fact; redemption which does redeem, pardon which does blot out sin, renewal which actually regenerates, salvation which completely saves. We have not in Christ the mere shadows of blessings, which charm the eye, yet cheat the soul; but real, substantial favours from God who cannot lie.

Christ has come to bring us grace and truth; that is to say, it is not the kind of truth which censures, condemns, and punishes; it is gracious truth, truth steeped in love, truth saturated with mercy. The truth which Jesus brings to His people comes from the mercy-seat. There is grace to God's people in everything that falls from the lips of Jesus Christ. His lips are like lilies dropping sweet-smelling myrrh. Myrrh in itself is bitter, but such is the grace of our Lord Jesus that His lips impart sweetness to it. See how grace and truth thus blend, and qualify each other. The grace is all true, and the truth is all gracious. This is a wondrous compound made according to the art of the Divine Apothecary; where else is grace so true, or truth so gracious?

Furthermore, grace and truth are blessedly balanced in Christ. He is full of grace; but, then, He has not neglected that other quality which is somewhat sterner, namely, that of truth. I have known many people in this world who have been very loving and affectionate, but then they have not been faithful; on the other hand, I have known men who were sternly honest and truthful, but they have not been gentle and kind; but, in the Lord Jesus Christ, there is no defect either way. He is full of grace which doth invite the publican and the sinner to Himself; but He is full of truth which doth repel the hypocrite and Pharisee. He does not hide from man a truth however terrible it may be, but He plainly declares the wrath of God against all unrighteousness. But when He has spoken ter-

rible truth, He has uttered it in such a gracious and
tender manner, with so many tears of compassion
for the ignorant and those that are out of the way,
that you are as much won by His grace as you are
convinced by His truth. Our Lord's ministry is not
truth alone, nor grace alone; but it is a balanced,
well-ordered system of grace and truth. The Lord
Himself is both King of righteousness and King of
peace. He does not even save unjustly, nor does
He proclaim truth unlovingly. Grace and truth are
equally conspicuous in Him.

But these qualities are also in our Lord to the
full. He is "full of grace." Who could be more so?
In the person of Jesus Christ, the immeasurable
grace of God is treasured up. God has done for
us, by Christ Jesus, exceeding abundantly above
all that we ask, or even think. It is not possible
for our imagination to conceive of anyone more
gracious than God in Christ Jesus; and there is an
equal fulness of truth about our Lord. He Himself,
as He comes to us as the revelation and manifestation of God, declares to us, not some truth, but
all truth. All of God is in Christ; and all of God
means all that is true, and all that is right, and all
that is faithful, and all that is just, all that is according to righteousness and holiness. There is
no truth hidden from us, that might have alarmed
us, nor anything that might have shaken our confidence in Christ; nor, on the other hand, is any
truth kept back which might have increased our
steadfastness. He said to His disciples, concerning
the glories of His Father's house above, "If it were
not so, I would have told you." Ask not, with Pi-
late, "What is truth?" but behold it in God's dear
Son. All truth and all grace dwell in Christ in all
their fulness beyond conception, and the two lie
in each other's bosoms for ever, to bless us with
boundless, endless joy and glory.

Our Lord Jesus Christ is also full of grace and
truth in this sense, that He truthfully deals with

matters of fact relating to our salvation. I know the notion of the world is that the salvation of Christ is a pretty dream, a fine piece of sentiment; but there is nothing dreamy about it: it is no fiction; it is fact upon fact. The Lord Jesus Christ does not gloss over or conceal the condition of man in order to secure his salvation. He finds man condemned, and condemned in the very worst sense, condemned for a capital offence; and as man's Substitute, He endures the capital penalty, and dies in the sinner's stead. The Lord Jesus views the sinner as depraved, yea, as dead in trespasses and sins, and He quickens him by His own resurrection life. He does not wink at the result of the Fall, and at the guilt of actual sin; but He comes to the dead sinner, and gives him life; He touches the diseased heart, and heals it.

To me, the Gospel is a wonderful embodiment of omnipotent wisdom and truth. If the Gospel had said to men, "The law of God is certainly righteous, but it is too stern, too exacting, and therefore God will wink at many sins, and make provision for salvation by omitting to punish much of human guilt," we should always have been in jeopardy. If God could be unjust to save us, He could also be changeable, and cast us away. If there was anything rotten in the God-made structure of our salvation, we should fear that it would fail us at last. But the building is secure, and the foundation is sure, for the Lord has excavated down to the solid rock. He has taken away all sentiment and sham, and His salvation is real and substantial throughout. It is a glorious salvation of grace and truth, in which God takes the sinner as he is, and deals with him as he is; yea, and deals with the sinner as God is, on the principles of true righteousness; and yet saves him, because the Lord deals with him in the way of grace, and that grace encourages a great many hopes, and those hopes are all realized, for they are based upon God's truth.

XXXVI. CHRIST'S FULNESS RECEIVED BY HIS PEOPLE

NOT only does John say that our Lord Jesus Christ is "full of grace and truth," but he adds, "and of His fulness have all we received." It is not one saint alone who has derived grace from the Redeemer, but all have done so; and they have not merely derived a part of the blessings of grace from Jesus, but all that they ever had they received from Him.

It would be a wonderful vision if we could now behold passing before us the long procession of the chosen, the great and the small, the goodly fellowship of the apostles, the noble army of martyrs, the once weeping but now rejoicing band of penitents. There they go! Methinks I see them all in their white robes, bearing their palms of victory. But you shall not, if you stay the procession at any point, be able to discover one who will claim to have obtained grace from another source than Christ; nor shall one of them say, "I owed the first grace I gained to Christ, but I gained other grace elsewhere." No, the unanimous testimony of the glorified is, "Of His fulness have all we received." My inner eye beholds the countless throng as the wondrous procession passes, and I note how every one of the saints prostrates himself before the throne of the Lamb, and all together they cry, " 'Of His fulness have all we received.' Whoever we may be, however faithfully we have served our Master, whatever of honour we have gained, all the glory is due unto our Lord, who has enabled us to finish our course, and to win the prize. '*Non nobis, Domine!'* is our cry; 'not unto us, O Lord, not unto us, but unto Thy Name be all the praise!' "

What a precious truth, then, we have before us, that all the saints in all ages have been just what we must be if we would be saved; that is, receivers! They did not any of them bring anything of merit to Christ, but they received everything from Him. If they, at this moment, cast their crowns at His feet, those crowns were first given to them by Him. Their white robes are wedding garments of His providing. The whole course of saintship is receptive. None of the saints above talk of what they gave to Jesus, none of them speak of what came of themselves; but, without a solitary exception, they all bear testimony that they were receivers from Jesus' fulness.

This truth casts mire into the face of human self-sufficiency. What! is there not one saint who had a little grace of his own? Is there not one of all the favoured throng who could supply himself with what he needed? No, not one. Did none of them look to the works of the law? No, they all went to Jesus and His grace, not to Moses and the law. Did none of them trust in priests of earthly anointing? Did none of them bow down before holy fathers and saintly confessors to obtain absolution? There is not a word said about any such gentry, nor even a syllable concerning appeals to saints and saintesses; but all the saved ones declare that they received grace and salvation direct from His fulness, who filleth all in all.

These receptive saints received very abundantly from Christ's fulness. They drew from an abundance, and they drew largely from it, as the words seem to indicate. It is worth while to notice the marvellous simplicity of the one act by which salvation comes to all saints. It is merely by receiving. Now, receiving is a very easy thing. There are fifty things which you cannot do; but, my dear friend, you could undoubtedly receive a guinea, could you not, if it were offered to you? There is not a rational man, or woman, or child, so imperfect in power as to be unable to receive. Everybody seems capable of receiving to any amount; and, in salvation, you have to do nothing but merely receive what Christ gives.

There is a beggar's hand, and if it be wanted to write a fair letter, it cannot do that, but it can receive alms. Try it, and the beggar will soon let you know that it can do so. Look at that next hand; see you not that it has the palsy? Behold how it quivers and shakes! Ah! but for all that, it can receive. Many a palsied hand has received a jewel. But the hand that I now see, in addition to being black, and palsied, is afflicted with a foul disease; the leprosy lies within it, and is not to be washed out by any mode of purification known to us; yet even that hand can receive; and the saints all came to be saints, and have remained saints, through doing exactly what that poor black, quivering, leprous hand can do. There was not in John any good thing but what he had received from his Master; there was not in the noble proto-martyr, Stephen, one grain of courage but what he had received from Christ; Paul, Apollos, Cephas,—all these had nothing but what they took from Him. If, then, they received everything from Christ, why should we hesitate to do the same?

All their grace came by receiving; so, dear reader, I put to you the question,—Have *you* received of the fulness of Christ? Have you come to Him all empty-handed, and taken Him to be your All-in-all? I know what you did at first; you were busy accumulating the shining heaps of your own merits, and esteeming them as if they were so much gold; but you found out that your labour profited not, so at last you came to Christ empty-handed, and said to Him, "My precious Saviour, do but give me Thyself, and I will abandon all thought of my own merit. I renounce all my giving, and doing, and working, and I take Thee to be everything to me." Then, friend, you are saved if that be true, for acceptance of Christ is the hall-mark of saints.

The fulness of God's grace is placed where you can receive it, where you can receive it now, for it is placed in Him who is your Brother, bone of your bone, and flesh of your flesh; it dwells in Him who loves to give it, because, as our Head, He delights to communicate grace to all the members of His mystical body. The plenitude of grace dwells in Him who is Himself yours; and since He is yours, all that is in Him is yours. You need not pray as if you had no inheritance in the blessing which you seek. Christ is the Trustee of the fulness of God, and the ownership of it is vested in His people; you have only to ask of Him, and He will give you that which is your own already. Why do you hesitate? How can you linger? The Father has placed His grace in Christ because it gratifies His love to His Son. It pleases the heart of the great God to see Jesus adorned with the fulness of Deity, and every time Jesus gives out grace to believers, the heart of God is thereby gladdened. How can you hesitate about receiving it if it pleases God for you to partake of it? You may go with high expectation of comfort, since Jesus Himself is honoured by your going to Him. He obtains glory by distributing of His fulness to empty sinners, who, when they receive grace, are sure to love Him; then, how can you think Him reluctant to bestow the gift which will increase His glory?

Thinking upon this subject brings to my mind right joyful memories of the hour when first these eyes looked to Christ, and were lightened; when I received pardon from His dying love, and knew myself forgiven. Have not many of my readers similar recollections? And since your conversion, is it not true that everything good you have ever had you have received from your Lord? What have you drunk out of your own cistern? What

treasure have you found in your own fields? Na-
kedness, poverty, misery, death,—these are the
only possessions of nature; but life, riches, fulness,
joy,—these are gifts of grace through Jesus Christ.
Are you accepted before God? Then, He has jus-
tified you. Have you been kept? Then, He has
preserved you. Are you sanctified? Then, He has
cleansed you by His blood. Do you know, by full
assurance, your interest in the Father's love? Then,
He gave you that assurance. All you have, and all
you ever will have, all that every saint who ever
will be born shall have, that is worth the having,—
all has been received, and will be received from
Christ's fulness.

Do you not know, too, that when you receive
from Christ, you gain by that very act? I am so
thankful that Christ has not put the fulness of
grace in myself, for then I should not require to
go to Him so often; or if I did go to Him, I should
not have an errand to go upon of such importance
as to justify me in seeking an audience; but now,
every time I go to Christ's door, I can plead necessity. We go to Him because we must go. When is
there an hour when a believer does not need to receive from Jesus? Go, then, beloved, to Him often,
since your going honours Christ, pleases God, and
is the means of soul-enrichment for yourselves.

XXXVII. Room for Christ Jesus

THE palace, the forum, and the inn, had no room for Christ; have *you* room for Him? "Well," says one, "I have room for Him, but I am not worthy that He should come to me." Ah! I did not ask about your worthiness; have you room for Him? "Oh!" says another, "I have an aching void the world can never fill." Ah! I see that you have room for Christ. "Oh, but the room I have in my heart is so base!" So was the manger at Bethlehem. "But it is so despicable." So was the manger a thing to be despised. "Ah! but my heart is so foul." So, perhaps, the manger may have been. "Oh, but I feel it is a place not at all fit for Christ!" Nor was the manger a place fit for Him, and yet there was He laid. "Oh! but I have been such a great sinner; I feel as if my heart had been a den of evil beasts." Well, the manger had been a place where beasts had fed.

I repeat the question,—Have you room for Christ in your heart? Never mind what your past life has been; He can forget and forgive. It mattereth not what even thy present state may be if thou sincerely mournest thy sinfulness. If thou hast but room for Christ, He will come, and be thy Guest. Do not say, I pray you, "I hope *I shall have* room for Him;" the Gospel message is, "Today if ye will hear His voice, harden not your hearts, as in the provocation;" "behold, now is the accepted time; behold, now is the day of salvation." Make room for Jesus! Make room for Jesus now!

"Oh!" saith one, "I have room for Him, but will He come to me?" Will He come? Do you but set the door of your heart open, do you but say,

"Jesus, Master, all unworthy and unclean, I look to
Thee; I trust in Thee; come Thou, and dwell within
my heart;" and He will come to thee, and He will
cleanse the manger of thy heart; nay, more, He will
transform it into a golden throne, and there He
will sit and reign for ever and ever. I rejoice that
I have such a free Christ, such a precious loving
Jesus to make known; One who is willing to find a
home in every humble heart that will receive Him.
Oh! it will be a happy day for you when you shall
be enabled to take Him in your arms, and receive
Him as the Consolation of Israel. You may then
look forward even to death with joy, and say, with
good old Simeon, "Lord, now lettest Thou Thy servant depart in peace, according to Thy Word: for
mine eyes have seen Thy salvation."

My Master wants room; and I, as His herald,
cry aloud, "Room for the Saviour! Room! Here is
my royal Master, have you room for Him? Here
is the Son of God made flesh, have you room for
Him? Here is He who can forgive all sin, have you
room for Him? Here is He who can take you up
out of the horrible pit, and out of the miry clay,
have you room for Him? Here is He who, when
He cometh in to your soul, will never go out
again; but will abide with you for ever, to make
your heart a heaven of joy and bliss through His
presence? Have you not room for Him?" That is all
He asks, room. Your emptiness, your nothingness,
your want of feeling, your want of goodness, your
want of grace,—all these will be but room for Him.

John tells us that, "as many as received Him, to
them gave He power to become the sons of God;"
and in the last great day, the Lord Jesus will say
to those on His right hand, "I was a stranger, and
ye took Me in." Is it not a strange thing that "He
was in the world, and the world was made by
Him," and yet He was a stranger in it? Yet it is not
a whit more strange than true; for, when He was
born, there was no room for Him in the inn. Inns

had open doors for ordinary strangers, but not for Him; for He was a greater stranger than any of those who were around Him. It was Bethlehem of David, the seat of the ancient family to which He belonged; but, alas! He had become "a stranger unto His brethren, and an alien unto His mother's children," and no door was opened unto Him.

Soon, there was no safe room for Him in the village itself, for Herod the king sought the young Child's life, and He must flee into Egypt, to be a stranger in a strange land, and worse than a stranger,—an exile and a fugitive from the land whereof by birthright He was King. On His return, and on His appearing in public, there was still no room for Him among the great mass of the people. He came to His own Israel, to whom prophets had revealed Him, and types had set Him forth; but they would not receive Him. "He was despised and rejected of men." He was the Man "whom men abhorred;" whom they so much detested that they cried, "Away with Him! Crucify Him! Crucify Him!" Jew and Gentile conspired to prove how truly He was a stranger; the Jew said, "As for this fellow, we know not from whence He is;" and the Roman asked Him, "Whence art Thou?"

Perhaps the strangest thing of all, and the greatest wonder of all, is that this Heavenly Stranger should be willing to be received by us, and that He should deign to dwell in our hearts. Such an One as Jesus in such an one as I am! The King of glory in a sinner's bosom! This is a miracle of grace; yet the manner of accomplishing it is simple enough. A humble, repenting faith opens the door, and Jesus enters the heart at once. Love shuts to the door with the hand of penitence, and holy watchfulness keeps out intruders. Thus is the promise made good, "If any man hear My voice, and open the door, I will come in to him, and will sup with him, and he with Me." Meditation, contemplation, prayer, praise, and daily obedience, keep the house in order for the Lord; and then follows the consecration of our entire nature to His use as a temple; the dedication of spirit, soul, and body, and all their powers, as holy vessels of the sanctuary; the writing of "Holiness unto the Lord" upon all that is about us, till our every-day garments become vestments, our meals sacraments, our life a ministry, and ourselves priests unto the Most High God. Oh, the supreme condescension of this indwelling of Christ! He never dwelt in angel, but He resides in a contrite spirit. There is a world of meaning in the Redeemer's words concerning His disciples, "I in them." May we know the meaning of them as Paul translates and applies them, "Christ in you, the hope of glory"!

The moment Christ is received into our hearts by faith, we are no longer strangers and foreigners, but fellow-citizens with the saints, and of the household of faith; for the Lord adopts us, and puts us among His children. It is a splendid act of Divine grace, that He should take us, who were heirs of wrath, and make us heirs of God, and joint-heirs with Jesus Christ. Such honour have all the saints, even all that believe on Christ's Name.

Then, when Christ is in us, we search out opportunities of bringing prodigals, strangers, and outcasts to the great Father's house. Our love goes out to all mankind, and our hand is closed against none; if so be we are made like to God, as little children are like their father. Oh, sweet result of entertaining the Son of God by faith! He dwells in us, and we gaze upon Him in holy fellowship; so that "we all with open face beholding as in a glass the glory of the Lord, are changed into the same image, from glory to glory, even as by the Spirit of the Lord."

"Love is of God; and every one that loveth is born of God, and knoweth God." May we daily feel the power of Jesus within our hearts, transforming our whole character, and making us to be more and more manifestly the children of God! When our Lord asks concerning us, "What manner of men were they?" may even His enemies and ours be compelled to answer, "As Thou art, so were they: each one resembled the children of a King." Then shall Jesus be admired in all them that believe, for men shall see in all the children of His great family the Divine Stranger's gracious and glorious handiwork.

XXXVIII. Christ's Two Appearings

THE two great links between earth and Heaven are the two advents of our Lord; or, rather, He is Himself, by His two appearings, the great bond of union between earth and Heaven. When the world had revolted against its Maker, and the Creator had been defied by His own creatures, a great gulf was opened between God and man. The first coming of Christ was like a bridge which crossed the chasm, and made a way of access from God to man, and then from man to God. Our Lord's second advent will make that bridge far broader, until Heaven shall come down to earth; and, ultimately, earth shall go up to Heaven.

Here, too, is the place for us to build a grand suspension bridge, by which, through faith, we ourselves may cross from this side to the other of the stormy river of time. The cross, at whose foot we stand, is the massive column which supports the structure on this side; and as we look forward to the glory, the second advent of our Lord is the solid support on the other side of the deep gulf of time. By faith, we first look *to* Jesus, and then look *for* Jesus; and herein is the life of our spirits. Christ on the cross of shame, and Christ on the throne of glory: these are our Dan and Beersheba, and all between is holy ground. As for our Lord's first coming, there lies our rest; the once-offered sacrifice hath put away our sin, and made our peace with God. As for His second coming, there lies our hope, our joy; for "we know that, when He shall appear, we shall be like Him; for we shall see Him as He is." The glories of His royal priesthood shall be repeated in all the saints; for He hath "made us unto our God kings and priests:" and we shall reign with Him for ever and ever.

At His first advent, we adore Him with gratitude, rejoicing that He is "God with us," making Himself to be our near Kinsman. We gather with grateful boldness around the Infant in the manger, and behold our God. But, in the anticipation of His second advent, we are struck with a solemn reverence, a trembling awe. We are not less grateful, but we are more prostrate, as we bow before the majesty of the triumphant Christ. Jesus in His glory is an overpowering vision for mortal man to behold. John, the beloved disciple, writes, "When I saw Him, I fell at His feet as dead." We could have kissed His blessed feet till He quitted us on Mount Olivet; but, at the sight of our returning Lord, when Heaven and earth shall flee away, we shall bow in lowliest adoration. His first appearing has given us eternal life, and that holy confidence with which we are looking forward to His glorious appearing, which is to be the crown of all His mediatorial work.

There are many contrasts between our Lord's first and second appearings, but the great contrast is, that, when He comes again, it will be "without a sin-offering unto salvation." The end and object of His first coming was "to put away sin." The modern babblers say that He appeared to reveal to us the goodness and love of God. This is true; but it is only the fringe of the whole truth. The all-important fact is, that He revealed God's love in the provision of the only sacrifice which could put away sin. Then, they say that He appeared to exhibit perfect manhood, and to let us see what our nature ought to be. Here also is a truth; but it is only part of the sacred design of Christ's coming to earth. He appeared, say they, to manifest self-sacrifice, and to set us an example of love to others; by His self-denial, He trampled on the selfish passions of man. We deny none of these things; and yet we are indignant at the way in which the less is made to hide the greater. To put the secondary ends of our Lord's first advent into the place of the grand object of His coming, is to turn the truth of God into a lie. It is easy to distort truth, by exaggerating one portion of it, and diminishing another; just as the drawing of the most beautiful face may soon be made a caricature rather than a portrait by neglect of the rule of proportion. You must observe proportion if you would take a truthful view of things; and in reference to the first appearing of our Lord, His chief purpose was "to put away sin by the sacrifice of Himself."

The great object of our Lord's coming here was not to live, but to die. He appeared, not so much to subdue sin by His teaching, or to manifest goodness, or to perfect an example for us to imitate, but "to put away sin by the sacrifice of Himself." That which the modern teachers of error would thrust into the background, our Lord placed in the forefront. He came to take away our sins, even as the scapegoat typically carried away the sin of Israel into the wilderness, that the people might be clean before the living God. Do not let us think of Jesus without remembering the design of His coming. I pray you, know not Christ without His cross, as some pretend to know Him.

We preach Christ; so do a great many more: but, "we preach Christ *crucified;*" so, alas! do not so many more. We preach, concerning our Lord, His cross, His blood, His death; and upon the blood of His cross we lay great stress, extolling much "the precious blood of Christ, as of a lamb without blemish and without spot." "Christ Jesus came into the world to save sinners," by putting away their sin "by the sacrifice of Himself." We will not deny, or conceal, or depreciate His master-purpose, lest we be found guilty of trampling upon His blood, and treating it as an unholy thing.

The putting away of sin was a Godlike purpose; and it is a wellspring of hope to us that, for this reason, Jesus appeared among men. If any of you are entertaining some so-called "larger hope", I would say to you,—Hope what you please; but remember, that hope without truth at the bottom of it, is an anchor without a holdfast. A groundless hope is a mere delusion. Wish what you will; but wishes without promises from God to back them, are vain imaginings. Why should you imagine or wish for another method of salvation? Rest you assured that the Lord thinks so highly of His Son's one sacrifice for sin that, for you to desire another, is a gross evil in His sight.

If you reject the one sacrifice of the Son of God, there remains no hope for you; nor ought there to be. Our Lord's plan of putting away sin is so just to God, so honouring to the law, and so safe for you that, if you reject it, your blood must be upon your own head. By once offering up Himself to God, our Lord has done what myriads of years of repentance and suffering could never have done for us. Blessed be the Name of the Lord, the sin of the world, which kept God from dealing with men at all, was put away by our Lord's death! John the Baptist said, "Behold the Lamb of God, which taketh away the sin of the world." God has been able to deal with the world of sinners in a way of grace, because Jesus died.

I thank our Lord, even more, because the actual sins of His own chosen—all those who believe on Him in every age—have been put away. These sins were laid on Jesus; and in Him God visited man for them. "He His own self bare our sins in His own body on the tree," and so put them away for ever. The putting away of my guilt as a believer was really, effectually, and eternally accomplished by the death of my great Substitute upon the bloody tree. This is the ground of our everlasting consolation and good hope through grace. Jesus did it, and did it alone, and did it completely; He did not only seem to do it, but He actually achieved the putting away of sin. He blotted out the handwriting that was against us. He finished transgression, and made an end of sin, and brought in everlasting righteousness, when once for all He died upon the cross.

I do not need, I hope, to linger here to warn you that it is of no use to expect that God will put away sin in any other way than that which, at so great a cost, He has provided. If sin could have been removed in any other way than by the death of His dear Son, Jesus would not have died. If there had been, within the range of supposition, any method of pardon except by the sacrifice of Himself, depend upon it Jesus would never have bowed His head to death. The great Father would never have inflicted the penalty of death upon the perfect One if it had been possible that the cup should pass from Him. He could never have imposed upon His well-beloved Son a superfluous pain. His death was needful; but, blessed be God, having been endured, it has once for all put away sin, and hence it will never be endured again.

Yet Christ Jesus will appear a second time; but not a second time for the same purpose as when He came before.

He will appear. The appearing will be of the most open character. He will not be visible simply in some quiet place where two or three are met together, in His Name, but He will *appear* as the lightning is seen in the heavens. At His first appearing, He was truly seen; wherever He went He could be looked at, and gazed upon, and touched, and handled. He will appear quite as plainly, by-and-by, among the sons of men. The observation of Him then will be far more general than at His first advent; for, as John says, "every eye shall see

Him." Every eye did not see Him when He came the first time; but when He comes the second time, all the nations of the world shall behold Him. They that are dead shall rise to see Him, both saints and sinners; and they that are alive and remain when He shall come shall be absorbed in this greatest of spectacles. Then Balaam shall find it true, "I shall see Him, but not now: I shall behold Him, but not nigh." Though the ungodly shall cry, "Hide us from the face of Him that sitteth on the throne," they shall cry in vain; for before His judgment-seat they must all appear.

His second appearing will be without sin. That is to say, He will bring no sin-offering with Him, for, having presented Himself as the one sacrifice for sin, there is no need of any other offering. When our Lord comes in His glory, there will remain no sin upon His people. He will present His bride unto Himself a glorious Church, not having spot, or wrinkle, or any such thing. The day of His appearing will be the manifestation of a perfect body as well as a perfect Head. "Then shall the righteous shine forth as the sun" when their Lord's countenance is "as the sun shineth in his strength." As He will be "without sin," so will they be "without sin." Oh, what a glorious appearing will this be;—a true appearing, yet the very opposite of the first!

If we are really expecting our Lord to come, we shall be concerned to have everything ready for His appearing. I sometimes see the great gates open in front of the larger houses in the suburbs; it usually means that the master is expected soon. Keep the great gates of your soul always open, ready for your Lord's return. It is idle to talk about looking for His coming if we never set our house in order, and never put ourselves in readiness for His reception. Looking for Him, means that we stand in a waiting attitude, as a servant who expects his master to be at the door presently.

Do not say, "The Lord will not come yet, and therefore I shall make my plans for the next twenty or thirty years irrespective of Him." You may not be here in the next twenty or thirty minutes; or, if you are, your Lord may be here also. He is already on the road; He started long ago, and He sent on a herald before Him to cry, "Behold, I come quickly." He has been coming quickly over the mountains of division ever since; and He must be here soon. If you are truly looking for His appearing, you will be found in the attitude of one who waits and watches, that when his Lord cometh he may meet Him with joy. Are you thus expecting Him?

I am afraid I shall only be speaking the truth if I say that very few Christians are, in the highest sense, *waiting* for the appearing of their Lord and Saviour. As to *watching*, this is still more rare than waiting. The fact is, even the better sort of believers, who wait for His coming, as all the ten virgins did, nevertheless do not watch, as the whole ten waiters slumbered and slept. This is a mournful business. A man, who is asleep, cannot be said to *look*; yet it is "unto them that look for Him" that the Lord is to "appear the second time without sin unto salvation." We must be wide-awake to look; we ought to go up to the watch-tower every morning, and look toward the sunrising, to see whether Christ is coming; and our last act at night should be to look out for His star, and ask, "Is He coming?" It ought to be a daily disappointment when our Lord does not come; instead of being, as I fear it is, a kind of foregone conclusion that He will not come just yet.

Many professing Christians appear to forget all about Christ's second coming; others drop a smile when we speak about it, as though it was a subject that belonged only to fanatics and dreamers. But ye, beloved, I trust are not of that kind. As ye believe really in the first coming and the one great sacrifice, so believe really in the second coming without a sin-offering unto the climax of your salvation. Standing between Christ's cross and His crown, between the cloud that received Him out of our sight, and the clouds with which He will come with ten thousands of His saints to judge the quick and the dead, let us live as men who are not of this world, strangers in this age which darkly lies between two bright appearings, happy beings saved by a mystery accomplished, and soon to be glorified by another mystery which is hastening on to its fulfilment. Let us, like that woman mentioned in the Revelation, have the moon under our feet, and keep all sublunary things in their proper place. May we even now be made to sit together in the heavenlies with Christ, that, when He appears, we may also appear with Him in glory! Amen.

Printed in the USA
CPSIA information can be obtained
at www.ICGtesting.com
LVHW040533221123
764422LV00003B/577

9 781948 648851